The Pyramid

MW01108297

15 Characteristics All Leaders Need In Order To Build a Successful, Long Term Business

By

Christopher Sopko

World's Best Business Books

2014

Copyright © 2014 by Christopher Sopko

All rights reserved. This book or any portion thereof may not be reproduced or used in any manner whatsoever without the express written permission of the publisher except for the use of brief quotations in a book review or scholarly journal.

First Printing: 2014

ISBN: 978-1505855395

World's Best Business Books
New York, NY   10001

www.chrissopko.wix.com/chrissopko

Table of Contents

Introduction

John Wooden was a legendary college coach that guided the UCLA men's basketball program from 1946 to 1975. During the years from 1964 to 1975 his record was 365 wins and 22 losses for a 94.3% winning percentage. During that 11 year period UCLA won 10 NCAA basketball championships. The next most number of championships by an individual coach is a tie at four between Adolph Rupp from Kentucky and Mike Krzyzewski at Duke. In his 29 years as a coach Wooden won over 80% of his games and no active college men's coach has a higher winning percentage. During the late 1960's his teams won 88 straight games, which is still a men's college basketball record.

Clearly, Wooden was a great basketball coach, an equally great leader of people, and from what his colleagues and ex-players say, a great person:

> *"[He] has a heart, brain and soul that have enabled him to inspire others to reach levels of success and peace of mind that they might never have dreamed possible on their own."* - **Bill Walton '74, UCLA Magazine (March 2007)**

> *"There's never been a finer man in American sports than John Wooden, or a finer coach."* - **Rick Reilly, CNN Sports Illustrated (March 14, 2000)**

> *"He wanted to win, but not more than anything ... My relationship with him has been one of the most significant of my life ... The consummate teacher, he taught us that the best you are capable of is victory enough, and that you can't walk until you crawl, that gentle but profound truth about growing up."* - **Kareem Abdul-Jabbar '69, "Kareem" (1990)**

1

"Wooden was a role model, not just as a coach and a wise man, but also for his modesty and character, and on how to age successfully. He was a legend in ways that go far beyond basketball. His personality, positivity, wisdom and attitude toward aging played important roles in his cognitive vitality. He also had a great sense of humor about life, and even death ... One of Coach's famous quotes was, 'When I am through learning, then I am through.'" - **Alan Castel, UCLA assistant professor of psychology, who interviewed Wooden about aging and memory in 2008**

As a young man I read Coach Wooden's autobiography, which contained a graphical model that he created to outline his theory on what it took to be successful as both a basketball player and in the game of life. I have included a copy below:

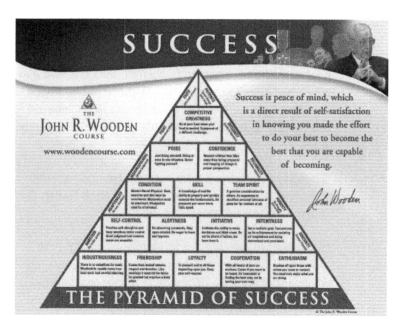

As you can probably tell from the title of this book, Wooden's chart resonated with me and caused me to think about what attributes and characteristics are necessary for someone to succeed in business.

Many of the characteristics in <u>The Pyramid of Business Success</u> are directly related to my upbringing in Cleveland, Ohio, where a Midwestern work ethic was instilled by the regional culture along with the strong, hard-working values of my parents, especially my father. For those of you familiar with the Midwest, it is filled with loyal, honest people that believe in the importance of family and getting paid a fair wage for a fair days work. Pragmatic may be the best way to describe them.

I graduated from college with a degree in education, but through life's many twists and turns ended up with a 30-year career in business – much of it spent working my way up to President of US operations for a multinational corporation headquartered in Denmark that has been around for over 120 years. Since 2000 I have worked as the President of three different international organizations, before deciding in 2013 to branch off on my own to start a private consulting company for small businesses as well as those involved in the life science and industrial equipment markets.

I credit my success to a lot of hard work and being able to surround myself with people who want to be great. Every one of my key managers who helped contribute to my success (and the success of these businesses) have all been honest, enthusiastic and demonstrated a tremendous amount of integrity every day.

Coupling my many years of successful business experience with the Midwestern work ethic provided me with the impetus to create this book.

A quick Google search shows there are hundreds of thousands, if not millions, of articles and books written about what it takes to be successful in business. Clearly, many other people have an interest in this topic as well. Many of them identify very specific business skills like "negotiating", being "good at numbers" or having "no fear of failure". What I couldn't find was a tool that really spelled out the core attributes and personal characteristics of successful business people; the type of people that others want to be around, that lead by example, and that time and again demonstrate long term success. In my opinion, even the most famous and well known books on this subject do not adequately cover the topic.

Due to the lack of complete information, I began to document and outline the critical behaviors and personal characteristics I feel are important and I narrowed them down to just 15 items. Many of these may appear to be quite obvious, but putting them into a graphical model enables everyone to easily review and educate themselves on what it takes to be successful. The end result is The Pyramid of Business Success and the concepts have application regardless of the markets or products being sold.

I truly believe that most organizations in today's environment will not be able to maintain long-term success if the business managers/owners do not demonstrate a significant portion of the attributes described in the upcoming chapters on a day-to-day basis. It should also be apparent that hiring people who have these skills or characteristics will have a positive effect upon the success of an organization, no matter where they may be placed on the ever-ubiquitous organization chart.

Most business owners cite "people" as their most important asset. Many companies spend millions of dollars teaching their team members new skills which can very often be a worthwhile investment. Sometimes, however, the training will be quite effective for one person and a total failure for another. Why is this the case? It may, in part, be due to the educational background and intelligence of the people involved. But I doubt this is the reason in most instances. My years of experience lead me to conclude that the reason is more closely related to the actual type of person that you have hired, rather than how smart they are. Some people will operate with integrity, put in the hard work necessary, and use their enthusiasm and competitive spirit to learn and become a master at what is being taught. Others without the same type of characteristics simply sit through the training programs without putting in much effort to actually internalize the subject matter. In my opinion, this is the primary reason why organizations see a variance in the efficacy of their educational programs. Obviously, this is just one example of why ALL employees need to have a strong alignment to the characteristics in this book.

The importance of a good match to the characteristics outlined in the book will become even more pronounced over the next few years. Take a look at how www.about.com described the latest group of people who are now beginning to play significant roles in the work force, often referred to as the "Millennials" or "Generation Y":

> "Millennials are individualistic, innovative, creative, celebrators of diversity, multi-taskers, and write their own rules. They appreciate a structured, supportive work environment with personalized assignments and interactive relationships with their supervisors. Millennials work well in a team environment and prefer to have close relationships with their supervisors to help them feel more confident and supported.
>
> Millennials also strive for balance in their work and personal lives and are unwilling to commit to jobs requiring long hours, evening, or weekend work. This may seem like a lack of commitment to those who have given their heart and soul to an organization but Millennials do value achievement and are confident in their abilities to produce within the confines of a regular work week. Millennials look to work in meaningful jobs where they can make an overall contribution to the bottom line of the organization, while feeling like they are really helping them meet their overall objectives and goals."

Only time will tell, but I am of the opinion that the Millennials described above will respond quite well to managers who demonstrate the characteristics of The Pyramid of Business Success on a daily basis.

Regardless of the "generation" being considered, it will always be up to the hiring team at any organization to find the right people who are a good match to the attributes in this book. Sadly, my experience tells me that not many organizations spend a lot of time uncovering this type of information. Time and time again I have seen companies focus the efforts of their interview process on skill sets and previous experience, while spending little time (if any) uncovering the truth about the candidate's basic characteristics and the type of person that they are at their very core.

Once you determine the attributes in this book are important, then it is up to you as a business owner/manager to find the right people that match these characteristics as closely as possible. It is also up to you to try and continually develop these characteristics in your team members on a daily basis.

As a tool, this book not only clearly defines these important characteristics, but it also provides a lot of ideas and techniques to develop the attributes throughout your entire organization, including any "Millennials" that you may have already hired.

Many successful long-term businesses have been built by people who do not have any type of *"work-life balance"*, and it is for this reason that you will not see this characteristic as an actual block in The Pyramid of Business Success. You will note, however, that it actually surrounds my model and I have created an entire chapter pertaining to the topic toward the end of the book. I believe that this concept will become increasingly important over the next 5 to 10 years, especially given the influence that members of "Generation-Y" will continue to play. I therefore felt compelled to include some thoughts on the matter that you may want to consider as you develop your business and leadership skills.

As with any pyramid, mine has been constructed from the ground up, with the most important items contained in its base. Without a strong base any pyramid will simply collapse, and the same can be said for The Pyramid of Business Success.

Business Success

WORK-LIFE BALANCE

Level 1 – The Must Haves - Integrity, the desire and drive for Hard Work, Enthusiasm, Resilience, and Personal Accountability, are specific characteristics that are ingrained in people during their earliest, developmental stages. You will be hard pressed to enhance these characteristics to their fullest potential if they do not already have a strong foothold at the very core of your being and in the people you bring into your organization. All of the items in the remaining blocks will be irrelevant if these core characteristics are not part of how you and your team act on a day-to-day basis.

Levels 2 to 5 – Other Key Characteristics- The rest of the levels in my Pyramid contain extremely important attributes such as being Goal Driven, Competitive, and a Team Builder to name just a few. Some of them are "standard" skills that can be taught once a person has joined your organization and these skills will be much easier to develop if the person in question already has a strong match to the characteristics at the base of the Pyramid.

Every chapter of this book includes examples that illustrate how and why these attributes are important and also how to further develop these skills. Most examples have been culled from my many years of experience, but I am also not too proud to admit that I have included a lot of fine words and brief summaries written by others that I uncovered during my research. In each scenario I have done my best to acknowledge the author when and where it was appropriate.

Some people may take a quick glance at the 15 items in The Pyramid of Business Success and wonder why important characteristics like honesty, dedication, or other very legitimate attributes (such as having a solid financial background or the importance of being focused on good product development) are not separate blocks in my pyramid. This is certainly a good question and for this I have three answers.

1. **A lot of choices** - There are many legitimate characteristics that help play a role in building a successful long term business. Someone who is "supportive", has the "ability to delegate", is "open-minded", and has a "sense of humor" are just a few of items that I considered to include as blocks in my pyramid. Obviously, they did not make my final cut, not because they are not valuable characteristics; but because I wanted to keep the number manageable and focused on the top 15 that "*I*" considered to be

important. You may disagree with my selections and it may spark discussions as to whether or not I missed any items. All in all, it will be a healthy situation, especially if it causes a business owner or manager to seriously evaluate their behavior and perhaps make some changes in how they do things on a daily basis.

2. **Similar characteristics** - Some characteristics are so closely related that I merged them together into one block. The characteristics of "Honesty" and "Integrity" have been consolidated into my first block called "Integrity". As you will note from reading the chapter, I chose to use the word "Integrity" because you can be honest and not act with integrity, but you cannot act with integrity and not be honest. Another example is the characteristic of "Dedication" which I have placed together with "Hard Work". You may notice this type of consolidation in many chapters, therefore I suggest that it may be quite difficult to determine if I have overlooked an item until each chapter of the book has been read and evaluated.

3. **Characteristics and not skills** – "Product development" and "sound financial acumen" are examples of skills that can be taught to virtually anyone and you may note that they are absent from this book. Are they important to running a successful business? Absolutely.

But I wanted to focus on important *personal* characteristics or attributes that are often overlooked in the business world. I wanted to identify them, explain their importance and help provide tools that can help you as an owner or manager to develop them to their fullest potential. I must admit that the chapter on being "goal oriented" contains information on a number of different planning tools; and one might make the case that these are also skills that can easily be taught. You would certainly be correct in this assessment, but I could not create a chapter on being goal oriented unless I also discussed the important relationship that must also exist on the planning side. This is the reason why I have included additional information on strategic planning, marketing, and other general planning devices for business.

The final chapter provides specific tools and suggestions that business managers can use in order to ensure that they are hiring the people that most closely match the attributes and skills I have in The Pyramid of Business Success.

As already cited, this book is geared toward business owners/managers, but I also hope that it can bring value to every person involved in the business world regardless of their role. If the information can help even one business be more successful or help to develop a stronger workforce and how they act on a daily basis, then I'll be a happy man!

I realize that some of the forms and graphs that are contained in this book may be a bit difficult to read since they were converted from color into black and white. For this reason, I have created a website that contains copies of each one for further review. The URL follows:

http://chrissopko.wix.com/pobs

Good luck!

"Become the type of leader that people would follow voluntarily; even if you had no title or position." **– Brian Tracy**

"Success is not a destination, but the road that you're on. Being successful means that you're working hard and walking your walk every day. You can only live your dream by working hard towards it. That's living your dream." **– Marlon Wayons**

"I don't know where we should take this company, but I do know that if I start with the right people, ask them the right questions, and engage them in vigorous debate, we will find a way to make this company great." – **Jim Collins**

Chapter 1 - Integrity

You can probably imagine that the first characteristic in my pyramid, "Integrity" is the most important block on my list and you would be right. Displaying integrity on a day-to-day basis is a critical pillar in building a successful business. The term is often used interchangeably with the word honesty, but unfortunately this is a mistake. As I mentioned above, and it's worth repeating, you can be honest and not display integrity, but you cannot display integrity and not be honest.

For this reason, I need to explain why I see a difference between the two starting with the importance of honesty. For most of us the concept and importance of being honest goes back to our earliest formative years. As a child, George Washington and his famous cherry tree was one of the first stories I remember hearing, even though historians tell us that it never really happened. For a variety of reasons, it was drummed into me at an early age that it was extremely important to be honest. Although I'm not perfect, I try to live my life with honesty as one of my guiding principles.

Unfortunately, not everyone got the same message as we are reminded on a seemingly daily basis of the business scams and crooks that prey on the good nature and gullibility of others. This book was not written to focus on the negative, but on how to develop and maintain a successful business over the long haul; and the cornerstone of it all is to continually act with honesty and integrity.

Honesty

Over the years I have heard countless people complain about their boss and not because they were too demanding, but because they could not be trusted. They were constantly being told one thing and then another would happen.

How many of us have people in our lives that constantly lie? If we do, then we have probably marginalized them as much as possible. We have realized that sifting through their lies is too much work, too time consuming, and much too frustrating. The business world is difficult enough without having to constantly try and decide if what you are hearing is truthful or not.

How can anyone successfully work with other people if they cannot be trusted, of if their word means nothing? What employee wants to follow a boss that cannot be counted on, and what manager wants to try and manage an employee that constantly lies?

For me, honesty encompasses at least three areas:

1. Honesty with your customers
2. Honesty with your colleagues, friends and family
3. Honesty with yourself

The quickest way to destroy a sale or a business relationship with a customer is to be dishonest. I have never met a customer that wants to buy a product from a dishonest vendor. EVER.

A valuable lesson

When I first started in sales, I sat in on a meeting with a large, prestigious retail firm with hundreds of stores scattered throughout the United States. During the lengthy discussion one of the sales people from our company began to speak and the first words out of his mouth were *"Can I be honest with you?"* I learned a valuable lesson that day because the customer blurted out *"no…I want you to fuckin' lie to me!"* Obviously, I quickly understood how much value this specific customer (as do all customers) placed upon hearing honest information from a sales person, but I also learned how a normal, relatively innocuous statement like "can I be honest with you" indicates to a customer that previous statements might have been lies.

Years later, I had a sales manager that used to say the same thing to me during many of our discussions. I relayed the above story to him and he quickly stopped using the expression. Take note of this in future business discussions. You will be amazed how often these words are used by sincere people who have not considered how their statements can be misinterpreted.

It's important to recognize, however, that not all types of dishonesty are actually nefarious in nature. Sometimes it can simply be that certain influential people in an organization are unable or unwilling to face the truth about what is happening in their markets or with their products. As a consequence, other people with a vested interest in the organization (managers) simply choose to keep quiet. We've all probably experienced a short tempered executive who flew off the handle because someone told them something they did not want to hear. I've even seen people threatened with their jobs because they had the gall to speak out about very legitimate business issues that needed attention.

This creates a situation in which senior managers may not be willing to point out an obvious hole in a strategy, or refuse to explain to a business owner how the product they are trying to sell is not competitive, because they are afraid! In certain ways it's understandable because no one wants to lose their job due to a petulant owner or manager. How sad is it that business decisions all over the world are being made because certain people with high level authority can't or won't handle the truth? How many companies suffer from poor results due to these situations?

I want every person within my organization to simply tell the truth about any given situation rather than lie. I make this clear to everyone in my organization and I state it unequivocally when I first start in a leadership role at a company. I believe that it is much better to admit that you did not follow up on something, or that you made a mistake somewhere along the line, rather than lie about the situation and attempt to cover it up. This enables us as intelligent human beings to assess our options and to figure out the best way forward.

Effects of not being honest

Lying about business situations gets in the way and hurts everything and everyone involved. Let's take an example of a sales person who has lied by telling his supervisor that he is still following up on an existing opportunity when in fact he has not done anything.

This one small lie about an opportunity can have a negative effect in multiple areas:

- It hurts the customer because they do not get the information or support that they want and deserve.
- It hurts the sales person because they are decreasing their chance at winning the sale and any bonus or commission that might be otherwise be paid.
- It hurts the management team because it gives an incomplete picture of where things legitimately stand, and it could force people into making a wrong decision.
- It hurts the marketing/promotional department because if the sale is ultimately lost due to poor follow up it may give them an incorrect understanding about pricing or the competitive landscape.
- It hurts product design and engineering because another lost sale gives an indication that the product may no longer be competitive rather than the result of a poor sales job.
- It financially hurts the company because of the potential for lost revenue and profits.
- Finally, it hurts the image of the company because a customer dissatisfied with a poor sales effort will most assuredly tell his or her friends about their bad experience.

As you can see, there are at least seven negative consequences from this one simple lie!

Just as we've been told all too often, bad news from unhappy customers travels fast. *The Huffington Post* posted a blog from Ian Altman. Its focus pertained to deceptive practices within sales organizations, but it can be readily applied to dishonesty in any business situation:

> *Many years ago, deceptive practices ran rampant in the sales profession. Salespeople used pressure, misleading tactics, and their own imbalance of information to coerce buyers into deals that the customer would later find were not in their best interest.*
>
> *Two hundred years ago, if something like that happened, the customer might share the story with his/her friends the next time they saw them in person.*
>
> *Eighty years ago, they might have even called their friends who had a phone, to share the story. However, they might not be 100 percent certain that they ended up with a bad deal. They might not have had enough facts to confirm their suspicion.*
>
> *But...fast forward to today, and the customer has at least as much information as the salesperson. If the customer has less than a positive experience, he or she can share it with the world before they even leave your sight (or site).*
>
> *Author Dan Pink describes this as a shift from Buyer Beware to Seller Beware. In short, being deceptive today can cost you that customer, and anyone they can reach via social media -- which could be the entire free world.*

Now, that's a pretty sobering thought.

On a personal note, I once had a potential customer that wanted to buy one of our products that I knew would not be sufficient for what they intended. I tried many times to convince them that they would be dissatisfied with the solution, but I unfortunately was not in a position to offer any better alternative. I ended up telling them that I could not in good conscience sell them the product that they wanted and they ended up buying from one of my main competitors.

At first they were a bit upset because I was clearly standing in the way of the decision that they had already made, but ultimately they understood. Thankfully, they returned to me for future purchases because I had turned out to be accurate in what I had told them. They were not happy with the solution they bought from my competitor and they wanted to deal with me because of the honesty I had displayed.

Honesty throughout an organization

If you want to have on-going, open, and honest communication with your employees, then you must remember to always deal with mistakes in a reasonable and professional fashion. If someone within your organization admits to making a mistake then you cannot explode on them or ridicule them in front of their peers. You must deal with these situations in a calm, business-like manner or else you'll create an environment where others will no longer want to tell you the truth. Your reaction as a manager is a key factor in creating an environment in which people will want to tell you the truth.

It's also imperative to note that the overall notion of being honest has to start from the very top of an organization and truly be part of the corporate culture, especially if you want it to be adopted by your entire team. History has shown us, however, that many organizations often overlook their obligations despite their best intentions and the fact that they are clearly spelled out in their corporate values statement.

A prime example of this is what has taken place over the past decade at General Motors; as detailed by *The Reuters News Agency* when they filed the following story:

> *"GM on Monday recalled 3.36 million midsize and full-size cars globally with ignition switches that can be jarred out of the "run" position, potentially affecting power steering, power brakes and air bags.*
>
> *The switch issue is similar to the defect linked to at least 13 deaths in an earlier, 2.6-million vehicle recall of Chevrolet Cobalts and other small cars.*
>
> *GM engineers first noted the Cobalt problem more than a decade ago, and GM's slow response to the switch issue triggered investigations within the company and by Congress and federal agencies.*
>
> *"The recall is just sort of the tip of the iceberg in terms of what has to be done" at GM, Senator Richard Blumenthal, a Democrat from Connecticut and one of GM's more vocal critics in Congress, said after Monday's recall.*
>
> *GM said the engineer who designed the defective Cobalt switches, Ray DeGiorgio, also designed the switches on the latest batch of recalled cars. DeGiorgio was fired after the earlier recall. He could not be reached for comment.*
>
> *GM has issued 44 recalls this year totaling about 20 million vehicles worldwide, which is more than their total annual U.S. vehicle sales. Of the recalls this year, nearly 6.5 million of the vehicles were recalled for ignition switch-related issues, including more than half a million Chevrolet Camaros on Friday.*

The automaker raised a recall-related charge for the second quarter to $700 million from $400 million. That takes GM's total recall-related charges this year to $2 billion."

Without going into too much detail, it's clear that at least one engineer was allegedly familiar with the on-going technical problems related to the ignition but chose to keep it a secret, which created a multi-billion dollar problem for General Motors. Was this lack of honesty isolated to a few people or endemic to a large portion of the organization?

According to Mary Barra the recently appointed CEO of General Motors, the fault lies not in a few bad apples, but in a true lack of values within the organization. Brian Dickerson from *the Detroit Free Press* reports the following:

"…instead of quarantining the cause of the ignition fiasco in some distant corner of GM bureaucracy, Barra traced the problem to a cultural dysfunction that she said had pervaded the entire organization.

"We had more of a cost culture," she said, stressing repeatedly that GM was "changing to a customer culture that focuses on safety and quality."

The treatment, she emphasized, was well under way, buttressed by changes in training and protocol at every level of the company. Still, her diagnosis was startling: GM's crisis had emerged not from the errors of a few errant bureaucrats, but from a company-wide failure of character."

The General Motors story is not over. Week by week more recalls are announced and the gloom hovering over the organization seems to darken.

During recent congressional testimony Ms. Barra acknowledged the need for radical change and seems willing to bet her career on fixing the situation as Dickerson points out further in his article:

> "…Barra's congressional interrogators were skeptical. "Isn't it true that throughout its corporate history, GM has represented to the driving public that safety has always been the No. 1 priority?" asked Rep. Bruce Braley, a fourth-term Democrat from Iowa.
>
> Braley, who served as president of the Iowa Trial Lawyer's Association before winning election to his state's congressional delegation, produced a promotional screwdriver that he said had been distributed by the automaker's dealers in 1994. He read the slogan embossed on its barrel: "Safety comes first at GM."
>
> He allowed the cross-examiner's time-honored coup de grace — "Were you lying then? Or are you lying now?" to hang unspoken in the charged hearing room.
>
> But Barra answered it just the same.
>
> "I can't speak to statements that were made in the past," she said, adding that she had never seen the screwdriver in Braley's hand. "All I can say is, that this is the way we're working now, the training that we've done — we've changed our core values."
>
> It's dangerous for any CEO to utter words like that unless she's prepared to enforce them. It's even more

dangerous to declare flatly — some would say absurdly — that cost will never again be a factor in deciding whether to replace a faulty GM part or product that jeopardizes customer safety.

And unless every ambitious junior engineer gets the message, Barra's pronouncements may one day sound as ironic, and as nakedly insincere, as the slogan on Braley's screwdriver.

But no slogan becomes a core value until someone in power stakes her professional life on it. And now Barra has.

Give GM's new CEO that much: In a world that esteems corporate leaders more for containing scandal than for confessing error, she's set a new standard for candor.

Maybe Barra has no choice. Maybe she is grandstanding too.

But if I worked for General Motors right now, I don't think I'd call her bluff.

Bravo to Barra! She has stepped in, recognized a huge cultural issue within her organization and is willing to do whatever it takes in order to rectify the situation. I think she has a huge challenge in front of her, but I truly wish her well.

A slippery slope

Losing your corporate and individual integrity isn't typically something that happens on a systemic and grandiose scale overnight. As with most things it starts small and builds from there. Cory Weinberg from *Business Week* wrote an article about a recent study that uncovered how easily dishonest acts can snowball in an organization:

"The same kind of slippery slope that Bernie Madoff said led to his $18 billion Ponzi scheme can make workers and companies vulnerable to scandal — unless managers snuff out ethical transgressions that may seem minor, write four business school professors in the study.

In what they say is the first empirical study on how unethical decisions compound over time, the researchers tested college students and professionals to see how they responded when they introduced cash incentives for cheating.

In one part of the study, published in the Journal of Applied Psychology, researchers asked two groups to look at a series of screens, each with two dot-filled triangles, and estimate which had more dots. The sets changed over time so that early on, more dots appeared in the left triangle, and later in the series, more showed up on the right. For one group, that change happened gradually. For the other, the shift was more sudden.

Researchers paid participants based on their estimates, with a higher payout for choosing the left triangle than the right, giving them an incentive to overstate the number of dots on the left. People in the group that gradually saw the pattern change were more likely to keep over-counting the left-triangle dots, even when there were starkly more on the right. The group that saw the pattern flip abruptly was more honest.

Conditions where incentives for little lies — just a couple of extra dots — slowly morphed into incentives for big ones — way too many dots — "more than doubled the rates of unethical behavior," write David Welsh of the University of Washington, Lisa Ordóñez of the University of Arizona, Deirdre Snyder of Providence College and Michael Christian of the North Carolina at Chapel Hill.

"Because of this rationalization process — what we call moral disengagement — people are more likely to slip into a pattern of behavior," Snyder says in a press release. "We call this the slippery-slope effect."

One reported Madoff quote helps capture the phenomenon, the study says: "Well, you know what happens is, it starts out with you taking a little bit, maybe a few hundred, a few thousand. You get comfortable with that, and before you know it, it snowballs into something big."

They also cite Kweku Adoboli, the UBS rogue trader; former New York Times reporter Jayson Blair, who was caught fabricating facts in his stories, and reporters who hacked phones for British tabloid News of the World as examples of individuals who succumbed to an ethical snowball effect.

Business schools will likely take note of the study. Soon after the financial crisis, many top programs infused ethical thinking into curricula to prevent future alumni from starting the next economic meltdown.

The researchers call on managers to prevent ethics breaches with measures like quickly condemning even small lapses before they compound. "More ethical behavior may result over time when employees are encouraged to be vigilant in identifying financial mistakes rather than creative in attempting to find new financial loophole.""

As I read this article, a few poignant memories rushed into my head from my childhood. I vividly remember my father telling me as a young boy that the act of stealing something was always the hardest the first time you did it. He told me that every time afterwards that it would get easier until you did it without even thinking about it. In his own way he was trying to warn me about the "slippery-slope effect" described above and it has now been supported by a scientific study. Obviously, it's important to ensure that your team members NEVER stray from honest, ethical behavior and this starts right from the top. If you display ethical and honest behavior on a daily basis as a manager/owner, then you will increase the likelihood of your employees doing the same. This study clearly indicates that if you avoid small acts of unethical behavior that you will minimize your chances of it growing into a larger, more dangerous situation.

Honesty with yourself

On a much smaller, but no less important level, you must also recognize that being honest with yourself is another key aspect to your long term success. If you can't give an honest evaluation of your skills and shortcomings then how can you ever expect to get better?

I once had a sales manager that declined to take part in some additional product training because she told me that she had already been trained and that any additional training would be counterproductive. I was relatively new to the organization and since she was one of my senior managers I believed her and let her forego the training session. Months later I visited a customer site with her and it quickly became obvious that some of her product knowledge was woefully inadequate. Not only had she been lying to me about her knowledge, but she was being dishonest with herself about her own ability. It was clear to me that this person did not want to put forth the effort to raise their skills. This lack of internal honesty also hurt her customers because she was ill prepared to have an intelligent discussion on how our product might help them.

If you really want to get better at anything then you need to have an accurate and honest assessment of where you currently stand. Sometimes being honest with yourself can lead to astonishing actions. That sales manager resigned soon after because she realized that she no longer wanted to put in the kind of effort it was going to take to succeed.

Although it was painful, it was the best decision for her and the organization. I wish it had gone another way, but at least the honesty she finally displayed led her to a difficult, albeit necessary decision.

Honesty is one of the most important characteristics to long term success in any and every business and that is why it plays such a significant role in this chapter.

This now takes us to integrity. As I identified at the beginning of this chapter, integrity is quite often used synonymously with the word honesty. Even as I wrote this book a lengthy debate with a few colleagues ensued as to whether or not they were one and the same thing.

Integrity

That's why it is crucial to provide a better explanation on the meaning of integrity and how it pertains to honesty. Integrity is actually a bit of a strange word because most of us understand what is meant when we hear about a person with integrity, but many would have a hard time defining the word.

Ask a friend or colleague to define the word integrity. I bet that nearly all of them will begin with the word honesty. One definition I enjoy is "the quality of being honest _and_ having strong moral principles; moral uprightness." Another is "soundness of character". I have also heard it described as a person's "consistency of actions" because a person with integrity will always handle situations in a professional and consistent manner.

Only time will tell, but given the data cited above I have the strong feeling that Mary Barra from General Motors is a person with a lot of integrity.

Although integrity is often linked very closely to honesty, members of certain business organizations can actually be 100% honest and truthful with their employees and customers, and still not display much integrity.

Here's an example:

Many garments sold in stores throughout the world clearly identify that they are produced in Bangladesh. Obviously, marking the garments accurately as to the country of origin is completely honest, but using these low cost providers that treat people similarly to slaves is in my opinion, certainly not an act that displays much integrity. Multi-billion dollar organizations no doubt make the decision to utilize these companies and facilities as a way to maximize their profits. While I certainly do not begrudge any organization for their desire to make a tidy profit, I do decry them for continuing to be involved in situations and in countries that time and time again show that they have little, if any regard for their workers.

A few years back a fire broke out at a garment factory in Dhaka Bangladesh that claimed 117 lives. Many popular western garment producers were using the facility to manufacture their inexpensive goods. Afterwards a few of them claimed ignorance and donated insufficient funds to third party organizations that were supposed to fix the situation. Unfortunately, *The New York Times* identified that one of the larger organizations actually played a significant role in blocking reforms that would require retailers to pay more for apparel in order to help Bangladesh factories improve safety standards. By any measure this is not the type of action that could even remotely be construed as having any integrity whatsoever.

Unfortunately, all pleas of ignorance soon began to ring hollow when approximately one year later the Rana Plaza, a commercial facility in Bangladesh collapsed. Some of the same popular garment manufacturers that had been involved in the situation with the Dhaka fire (including the one that blocked reforms) also utilized this facility to produce their low cost products. Sadly, a month later the death toll was finalized at over 1,100 people! Unfortunately, it is now considered to be the most deadly garment factory accident in history. Honesty and integrity certainly did not go hand-in-hand in this instance.

The Huffington Post identified the following quote as being attributed to Pope Francis:

> *A headline that really struck me on the day of the tragedy in Bangladesh was that these people were 'Living on 38 euros a month'. That is what the people who died were being paid. This is called slave labor; the pope was quoted as saying at a private mass.*
>
> *Today in the world this slavery is being committed against something beautiful that God has given us -- the capacity to create, to work, to have dignity. How many brothers and sisters find themselves in this situation!" he said.*
>
> *Not paying fairly, not giving a job because you are only looking at balance sheets, only looking at how to make a profit. That goes against God!*

Again, I have no problem with any organization doing as much as they can to maximize profits as long as it is done in an ethical fashion. Given what I have been able to uncover about this situation, I struggle to see the ethics and integrity displayed by the organizations that continue to utilize what Pope Francis calls "slave labor".

Some might argue that all organizations, especially those that are publicly traded, are driven by maximizing profits and that they are literally forced into these decisions by market pressures.

But this is nothing but an excuse.

Publicly traded companies that act with integrity

Many large, publicly traded organizations operate in an ethical fashion yet still perform quite well from a financial standpoint. PepsiCo, the parent company for Pepsi, Dorito's, Tropicana and many other well-known brands around the world, has been selected as one of the most ethical companies in the world by two well known, reputable organizations called the Ethisphere Institute and the Swiss company called Covalence, which publishes its Ethical Quote rankings.

Surely, PepsiCo must be faced with similar pressures to cut costs and drive profits, yet they somehow manage to operate in an ethical fashion. Obviously, being cited in this way by multiple international organizations is a clear indicator of an organization that operates with integrity. This doesn't appear to be hurting them in any way as they have now surpassed rival Coca Cola in total revenue.

Another example of corporate and individual integrity came to light during the unfortunate situation regarding the Malaysian Airliner that was lost without a trace in 2014. In case you are not familiar, Malaysian Airlines Flight 370 was flying from Kuala Lumpur to Beijing and suddenly and inexplicably lost contact with air traffic controllers. At the time of this writing many months have passed and the aircraft and/or its wreckage have still not been found. It was as if the aircraft and its 227 passengers had simply vanished from the face of the earth.

Inmarsat, an international company that provides satellite services to many different industries including aircraft operators, has been an instrumental ally in current attempts to locate the missing Malaysian flight. As part of their ongoing efforts they came to the realization that the airline industry would be better served by providing additional detail that was readily available from their satellite systems. *Reuters* filed the following report:

> *... Inmarsat, the firm whose satellites helped track the final route of missing Malaysian Airlines airliner MH370, confirmed that it would offer a free, basic tracking service to passenger airlines globally.*
>
> *The company said that the service would be offered to all 11,000 commercial passenger aircraft which are already equipped with Inmarsat satellite connection, comprising virtually 100 percent of the world's long haul commercial fleet.*
>
> *"In the wake of the loss of MH370, we believe this is simply the right thing to do," Chief Executive Rupert Pearce said.*
>
> *"This offer responsibly, quickly and at little or no cost to the industry, addresses in part the problem brought to light by the recent tragic events around MH370."*

In this instance, Inmarsat and Pearce certainly appear to be acting with a tremendous amount of integrity. Obviously, organizations such as Inmarsat are set up to make a profit, yet Pearce made a corporate decision to "do the right thing" and provide a service to an entire industry for free.

Lip service

Many organizations create elaborate compliance programs in order to try and develop a sense of ethics and integrity in their business. Most organizations do this because they truly want to operate in a forthright fashion as well as avoid any of those nasty governmental fines. Others simply put forth these programs as a way to cover themselves from a legal standpoint. They create internal training programs that are nothing but lip service and still go about operating in unethical, and at times, illegal ways.

As an example, Neil Getnick from the *International Business Times* published an article that began in the following fashion:

> *"The insider trading indictment of SAC Capital Advisors and GlaxoSmithKline's (NYSE: GSK) massive bribery scandal in China are just two recent cases revealing a business culture in which legal compliance programs appear to have met with spectacular failures. SAC bragged about having a "strong culture of compliance," yet it now faces insider trading charges on an unprecedented scale in the hedge fund industry. And Glaxo's internal compliance efforts failed to uncover a $450 million bribery scheme that the giant drug company has now admitted. "*

How sad.

These are just two examples of multi-billion dollar organizations that simply thumb their noses at the law by taking part in bribery schemes and insider trading. Honesty and Integrity...*not so much!*

On a more personal note, I once had a friend that worked for a publicly traded organization that had its corporate headquarters in the US. One of its international subsidiaries continued to sell product to Iran even though the products were definitely on a list of prohibited items. My friend had recently been "educated" by this group on the dangers of breaking the law in this fashion and they were all encouraged to report any violations of which they might be aware. Unfortunately, she had the stupid notion (at least within this organization) to do as she was trained, and ask their internal corporate counsel if what they were doing by continuing to sell products to Iran was legal.

Needless to say, her queries created quite a stir and sadly she was soon out of a job. Obviously, this publicly traded company was more concerned about profits than following the law and they were willing to sacrifice the career of a loyal employee to keep things quiet. I'm sure that the company can come up with a myriad of reasons why she was terminated and none of them would have to do with her queries about the sale of products to Iran. I must point out that she was a 17 year veteran within this organization who had been promoted multiple times, and who had a performance record that was without blemish. It must be sheer coincidence that her downfall began immediately after she had the audacity to ask a question about products being potentially sold in an illegal fashion.

Even after this unfortunate situation occurred my friend didn't regret her actions and I see this as a true sign of her integrity. Strangely, she was actually trying to help the company and her payment was a boot out the door. It makes me wonder how long an organization can continue to do these things before they catch up to them, but it's always encouraging when individuals still have the wherewithal to make a stand on what they know to be wrong.

Like the recent activity from Inmarsat and from the friend I described above, I like to refer to acts of integrity as simply "doing the right thing". Throughout my career I have felt that it is actually a very simple principle. I believe that to be a successful manager that you need to look at each and every situation and simply base your actions on "what is the right thing to do here?" It may be allowing a single mother to arrive 15 minutes late every day so that she can take her daughter to school. It might mean giving someone time off to be with a sick child or to visit a loved one in the hospital. It might mean fixing a piece of equipment for free that is five days out of warranty. It might also be Mary Barra standing up to acknowledge the lack of integrity within her organization and taking the necessary steps to fix the situation.

In my opinion, it is these types of actions that develop respect throughout an organization. Granted, the decision to operate in an honest fashion will not always be easy, but living your goal to be a person of integrity and to do the right thing will help build an atmosphere of trust and make the people on your team want to be at work!

How to develop your honesty and integrity

If integrity is not already part of your makeup it will be difficult to develop. You most certainly will not be able to expect this from your employees if it is not something that you practice every day. This doesn't mean that you shouldn't try to improve in this area, which is the reason why I am providing some suggestions on things you can do as a business owner or manger to help strengthen your integrity and in helping your employees develop it as well.

- **Your decision and commitment** - Make a clear decision as to whether or not integrity has any place in your life. If not, then continuing to read this book may be a waste of time.
- **Accurate reflection** - Reflect on your life and your actions and how you truly act on a day-to- day basis. You must be BRUTALLY honest with yourself if you ever want to improve. This type of change through self-evaluation will become more effective over time. If you are the type of person that has made a habit of lying and cheating to get ahead, then change will be difficult, but the first step is recognition and acknowledgement.
- **An internal voice** - Before you make any significant decision ask yourself if what you are considering would be viewed by others as an act of integrity. You may want to internally visualize a "world expert" in ethics and integrity that you can mentally ask for guidance.
- **Be transparent** - Don't be afraid to admit your shortcomings or when you are wrong. Too often this is

one of the key reasons why people avoid acting with honesty and integrity. They are afraid to admit that they have made a mistake or dropped the ball so they attempt to cover up the situation. Being transparent, "warts and all" is one of the first things you need to accomplish on your goal to developing integrity.

- **The right people** - Surround yourself with people that continually display integrity. This is the surest way of developing integrity within your life. Your discussions with these people will begin to let you understand what integrity truly is and how you can build it into your life as well. Ask them for their help if you are struggling with determining the best course of action.
- **Feedback** – Seek feedback from people you trust after you have made a significant decision to ensure that you acted with integrity. If it turns out you made a mistake, then take immediate steps to rectify the situation and apologize to those involved.

Management Checklist

- ✓ Do I continually stress to my team the importance of acting with honesty and integrity on a daily basis?
- ✓ Does my team see me leading by example in dealing with every business situation with true integrity and in an honest fashion? In other words do I *do the right thing* every day?
- ✓ Have I created an environment of open communication that enables differing opinions and honest communication?
- ✓ When I interview a potential employee do I spend time trying to uncover how much value they place on honesty and integrity?
- ✓ If someone on my team makes a mistake do I deal with it in a professional fashion or do I get angry?

If the answers that you provide to these questions don't readily illustrate that you act with honesty and integrity, then you need to identify what steps you'll take to fix the situation. This is one of the most fundamental parts of building a successful, long term business and without it the rest of the blocks in The Pyramid of Business Success will soon begin to crumble.

"If you have integrity, nothing else matters. If you don't have integrity, nothing else matters." – **Alan K. Simpson**

"Have the courage to say no. Have the courage to face the truth. Do the right thing because it is right. These are the magic keys to living your life with integrity." - **W. Clement Stone**

"A true test of a person's character and integrity is what they do when no one is watching" – **John Wooden**

Chapter 2 - Hard Work

Although this chapter is simply entitled Hard Work, it could easily be expanded to include two other items: "A desire to be great" and "dedication". These concepts are all so heavily intertwined from a business standpoint that it is almost impossible to separate them. Most people accept that it takes a tremendous amount of hard work to build and maintain a successful, long term business. I firmly believe, however, that an individual will not be able to maintain a sustained level of hard work unless that person has a burning desire to be great AND a dedication to the organization or task at hand.

Hard work doesn't simply mean doing things in the most difficult fashion. Working hard and not smart is a waste of time. When I use the term hard work I mean being diligent to the task at hand. To stay at things until they are completed. If you're a business manager it means putting in the hours to ensure that nothing falls through the cracks, that your customers (both internal and external) are happy, and that you are preparing your organization to compete and be successful over an extended period of time. If you're in a sales position it means that you will continue to study the details and specifications about your new product until you can discuss them intelligently and without hesitation.

Examples of hard work

I don't want over run this book with sports analogies, but information about our current athletic superstars is readily available and certainly makes it easy to illustrate a lot of points about hard work, dedication, and the desire to be great.

Hank Haney, the swing coach of Tiger Woods during six of his major wins, wrote about Tiger's work ethic in his book called the "Big Miss". In it he outlined his daily workout:

1. Wake up at 6 am and work out for two hours
2. From 8-9 shower and eat breakfast
3. From 9-10:30 hit balls at the range
4. 10:30 – 11 practice putt
5. Play as many as nine holes until noon
6. 12-1 Lunch
7. 1-2 Short game work
8. 2-3:30 hit balls at the range
9. 3:30- 4:45 play nine holes
10. 4:45 – 6 practice putting
11. 6-7 Shoulder exercises and stretching

Now some of you may be thinking, hey it's golf, how much hard work is that? Of course, in a certain respect you are correct. But how many of us have this type of dedication to our job? How many of us practice and develop our skills like this every day? Tiger Woods is arguably the best golfer that ever lived and yet he still puts in this kind of effort and hard work – every day! Why? Because he knows that if he doesn't then he stands no chance of reaching his ultimate goal of winning more major championships than Jack Nicklaus.

There are many other famous people with an incredible work ethic:

Roy Halladay – The recently retired baseball pitcher for the Toronto Blue Jays and Philadelphia Phillies was reported to work out for 90 minutes each day before his team mates even made it to the ballpark. It was said that others who tried to duplicate his work outs could not make it half way without quitting.

Marie Curie – Another famous example of dedication and hard work comes from evaluating the life of Marie Curie. Many of you may know her name, but few might know that she was the first European woman to earn a doctorate in science and the first female professor at the University of Paris.

She was also the first woman to win a Nobel Prize and the first person to earn the esteemed prize in two different disciplines. Unfortunately, she was a woman in Poland during a time when getting an education for a female was officially forbidden.

In the late 1800s, women were not admitted to most European universities. Amazingly, many young people like Curie created something they referred to as the "floating university". The floating university enabled them to hold secret night classes in private homes and to frequently change locations to keep from being uncovered. Intellectually enlightened professors were kind enough to help them study science and mathematics. They also conducted secret lab research and developed their own library at great peril. Over time, thousands of young women attended this underground university, and it ultimately became a source of pride throughout Poland.

Curie ultimately moved to Paris at which time she was permitted to continue her studies at an accredited university, but her previous experiences and difficulties in gaining her early education had instilled in her an intense work ethic and an unwavering resolve.

Curie is not just an icon because of her efforts as a chemist, but also because of her ability to confront obstacles head on. Additionally, the hard work and dedication that she continually displayed are perhaps equally inspiring as her achievements.

Frederick Douglas - Another fine example of hard work and determination. Rising from the shackles of slavery, Douglas taught himself to read by interacting with white children and struggling with any printed material he could find. In 1883 Douglas escaped from slavery to Massachusetts and rose to prominence as an author, orator and most importantly an abolitionist. After the Civil War, Douglas served as the President of the Freedman's Savings Bank and became Chargé d'Affaires for the Dominican Republic. He also accepted an appointment as United States Marshal for the District of Columbia and was the first African American to be nominated for Vice President of the United States, as Victoria Woodhull's running mate on the Equal Rights Party ticket.

Obviously, this courageous man could never have risen to the heights that he did if it were not for his tremendous desire and hard work. He is quoted as saying that if a person has *"ordinary ability and opportunity, we may explain success mainly by one word and that word is WORK! WORK!! WORK!!! WORK!!!!"*

The examples above illustrate true dedication, hard work, and the benefits that can be realized from such efforts.

Conversely, I'd like to share another example of hard work, but certainly not smart work. During the summer while I was in college I worked at a golf course cutting greens, mowing fairways and doing general cleanup each day. It was a good college job that kept our team outdoors, in the sunshine and helped develop a lot of camaraderie that remains to this day. We had an interesting mix of five 19 and 20 year olds working their way through college and five full time people who had chosen this type of work as their livelihood.

One day a leak sprung up in the middle of a fairway and the "college kids" were assigned the task of finding the specific spot where the leak had started. We were given a few shovels and told to hand dig the area to a depth of about 3 feet to find the buried and obviously, leaking pipe. After about 30 minutes of this arduous work I asked one of the full-time and more senior workers if we could use the front end loader that had a back hoe to remove the majority of the dirt. He immediately began screaming at me that college kids were all lazy and afraid of hard work. He denied my request and we were therefore forced to continue with our manual efforts. As small as this incident was, it stuck with me as a clear example of working hard, but not smart. Within 15 minutes we could have had the dirt removed if we'd been allowed to use the back hoe. Instead we dug for hours in the mid-day sun because one misguided person could not understand the difference.

Legitimate hard work as a venue for success is a staple throughout the sports world. An old and very wise football coach named Woody Hayes made a commencement speech to graduates of Ohio State in 1986 in which he talks about its' importance. An excerpt follows:

> "In football, we always say, "That other team can't beat us. We have to make sure that we don't beat ourselves." And that is what a person has to do, too - make sure that they don't beat themselves. It takes an awful big man to beat you. So many times I've found people smarter than I was. I found them in football - bigger, they could run faster, could block harder, they were smarter people than I.
>
> But you know what they couldn't do? They couldn't outwork me. They couldn't outwork me! And I ran into coaches that I coached against who had a much better background than I did, knew a lot more football than I did, but they couldn't work as long as I could. They couldn't stick in there as long as I could.
>
> Of course my health was good. And I had a wonderful wife who put up with that - she'd allow me to stay and work. And I had great associations with my coaches. There was no one who had better people than I did, or better football players. And, we outworked the other teams. "

Even though he was speaking about football his statements certainly have utility in the business world. Too often during my career I saw individuals who were too lazy to put in the extra effort to fix a problem, win a sale, or make a customer happy.

Unfortunately, if an organization has too many people like this then they will not be around long. They will simply fade away as another failed business.

The business world is difficult enough without shooting yourself in the foot by not at least working hard. According to the Small Business Administration, only 44% of new businesses make it to the fourth year. It certainly does not apply to all of them, but how many might have been saved if every member of the team worked hard, had a desire to be great, and were dedicated to their job?

A desire to be great

As I cited at the beginning of this chapter, hard work is one thing that many people can and will do on a short term basis. I doubt, however, that many people will want to consistently put in the hard work necessary to truly be successful unless they also have an internal desire to be great! The two go hand in hand, and you cannot have one without the other. There MUST be a desire and passion to achieve long term success day in and day out, and you either have it or you don't!

Michael Jordan and Tiger Woods are prime examples of people who have an insatiable drive to be great. This drive enabled them to put in the countless hours of hard work necessary for them to be dominant in their sport. It is also what is needed to push business people to get better at their profession. To learn everything they need to know about their products, markets and competitors. It is a burning desire to simply be better than everyone else.

I have heard estimates that if you truly want to be great at something then it will take 10,000 hours of practice. This means that at two hours a day it will take you nearly 14 years of practicing to attain greatness! Obviously, not many people will put in this type of hard work without true dedication and a desire to be great.

Do you think that Bill Clinton had a desire to be great? He started out dirt poor as did Barack Obama. What about Amelia Earhart, Warren Buffet, or Steve Jobs? These people are all considered great because of their drive, determination, and ultimately the success they achieved. If you want to build a successful organization then you need to seek out people that have an internal drive to be great AND who are willing to work hard to get there!

One of the best examples of a desire to be great, coupled with the willingness to work hard, and unfailing dedication comes to us from the early part of the 20th century, which follows:

> *Thomas Edison is one of the best known inventors the US has ever produced, if not the world. The study of his background has understandably spawned countless articles and books that detail his miraculous life and career. He is credited with having invented the first commercially viable incandescent light bulb, an automated telegraph machine, the phonograph, and early versions of the motion picture camera. All in all he has over 1,000 patents to his name.*

> *Few people, however, know the story of Edwin Barnes. Born in 1878 in Wisconsin, this young man developed an overwhelming desire to become a partner with the already famous Thomas Edison. Unfortunately, he was a man of little means, had meager clothing, and could not even afford the train trip to get to where Thomas Edison had set up shop in New Jersey. Additionally, he had absolutely no technical background, yet he never wavered from his goal.*

> *In 1905 he arrived at Menlo Park, walked into the office and announced to everyone including Thomas Edison that he was there to become a business partner with the famous Mr. Edison. It is important to note, that he did not announce that he wanted to work for Mr. Edison, but*

that he wanted to be a partner with Mr. Edison. The other workers took one look at the man and began to laugh at him hysterically. Who was this poor looking man to march into their facility and make such a statement? It had to be a joke! Thomas Edison, on the other had did not find it funny and saw something in the man that intrigued him. What he saw was a man with desire and obvious determination. He hoped to utilize these characteristics to help grow his organization and quickly offered the man a job.

Unfortunately, for Edwin C. Barnes the job he received was not in the research group as he had hoped, but as a floor sweeper! Being an irrepressible man, Barnes recognized that he was not really getting a job as a floor sweeper, but that he would be getting paid to meet influential and powerful people all the while getting to know Edison and what made him tick. It would also get him the chance to display his work ethic and learn as much as possible about the technology that was all around him.

After two years Barnes seized upon an opportunity to show his stuff. Edison had been working for many years on a dictating machine and he was finally ready to commercialize the product. Many senior members of his team, however, were not convinced that the product would be viable and expressed little interest in helping Edison sell it.

Barnes on the other saw things differently. He recognized that this new invention could help executives dictate information at any time of the night and day, for playback at a later time. This freed up the executives from having a stenographer nearby to record their thoughts. Barnes realized the time savings and how such an invention could increase profits for nearly every business throughout the world.

Barnes took the time to create his own marketing plan and approached Edison with the idea of letting him sell his dictation machine. So impressed was Edison by Barnes enthusiasm and desire that he agreed to his proposal. Within months Barnes had sold thousands of the dictation machines and Barnes was given a financially lucrative contract to distribute the product throughout America. At a very early age Barnes became a millionaire and he was considered by many to be the most successful salesperson ever employed by Thomas Edison.

As far as I can tell Mr. Barnes and Mr. Edison never actually became partners, but they remained close associates until Edison died in 1931. During their 25 years together, Barnes became wealthy, but his greatest sense of accomplishment came from his knowledge that he helped thousands of people live happier and more productive lives.

Wow! Wouldn't it be wonderful to surround yourself with a whole team of people like Edwin C. Barnes? What if you could have an entire group of employees with this type of hard work and determination? Imagine the success you could achieve!

Bill Gates is another example of hard work coupled with a desire to be great. He was born in Seattle in 1955 and came from a family that constantly encouraged competition. One family friend said that *"it didn't matter whether it was hearts or pickleball or swimming to the dock ... there was always a reward for winning and there was always a penalty for losing."* Clearly, this type of background helped to develop the young Gates into an individual with an unquenchable desire to succeed.

In his early teens Gates and the friends sought time programming mini computers, one of which belonged to a company called Computer Center Corporation (CCC). Soon afterwards the four pals were caught exploiting bugs in the operating system in order to obtain free computer time, and were banned from further use. At the end of the ban they somehow actually convinced CCC to give them free computer time in exchange for their services in finding additional bugs.

At the age of 17, Gates and Paul Allen formed a company called Traf-O-Data to make traffic counters on one of the earlier forms of Intel processors. By 1973, Gates took a new position as a congressional page in the US House of Representatives. During that same year he took the SAT test and received a score of 1590 out of 1600' and soon after he enrolled in Harvard.

Wikipedia goes on to identify the origins of Microsoft in the following fashion.

> *After reading the January 1975 issue of Popular Electronics that demonstrated a product called the Altair 8800, Gates contacted the manufacturer called Micro Instrumentation and Telemetry Systems (MITS), the creators of the new microcomputer, to inform them that he and others were working on a BASIC interpreter for the platform. In reality, Gates and his friend Paul Allen did not have an Altair and had not written any code for it; they merely wanted to gauge MITS's interest.*
>
> *MITS president Ed Roberts agreed to meet them for a demo, and over the course of a few weeks they developed an Altair emulator that ran on a minicomputer, and then the BASIC interpreter. The demonstration, held at MITS's offices in Albuquerque was a success and resulted in a deal with MITS to distribute the interpreter as Altair BASIC. Paul Allen was hired into MITS, and Gates took a leave of absence from Harvard to work with Allen at MITS in Albuquerque in November 1975. They named their partnership "Micro-Soft" and had their first office located in Albuquerque. Within a year, the hyphen was dropped, and on November 26, 1976, the trade name "Microsoft" was registered with the Office of the*

*Secretary of the State of New Mexico. Gates never
returned to Harvard to complete his studies.*

It is clear from the above information that Bill Gates must have
had a really strong and burning desire to be great. He studied
situations and took advantage of each one to further his
knowledge and chances of success. His story is as of yet
unfinished, but without a doubt he is a true American success
story.

Any organization would do well to hire people like Edwin C.
Barnes and Bill Gates. Their desire to be great, determination,
hard work, and focus brought each of them undeniable success
and obviously contributed to building large, tremendously
successful organizations.

If you are a business manager, then you need to find people that
not only say they want to be the best, but can also demonstrate
during an interview how they have incorporated this search for
greatness into their lives. It can certainly be a fine line, but
please do not confuse the desire to be great with arrogance. I
firmly believe that people that want to be great do not need to be
self-centered, cocky, or hard to manage.

I have an acquaintance that runs a real estate agency. When he
advertises for sales people he flat out states that he only wants
people who want to be great. Lazy people need not apply. As a
business owner/manager it is important for you to find these
types of people. When you interview a potential candidate, ask
them about greatness and what it means to them. If they have
never thought about it, then they do not have this desire.

Don't surround yourself with mediocre people because they will
make you mediocre as well.

It is also important for a business manager to recognize that
there is a difference between a job and a career. A job is
something that we might have worked at during the summer

break from college. Typically, it was a minimum wage position that we only did because we needed some money for tuition or to put gas in the car. Very few people are dedicated to this type of job. They show up every day because they have to.

A person with a career has a different attitude and is typically dedicated to ensuring their success. A career is something that is important to the individual and to them it's not just a job. It's a source of pride that requires effort, study and provides a sense of well-being when things go well. A person who is dedicated to their career is often times very concerned when things are not going well within their organization or with their sales efforts. They're very committed to the task at hand and truly want to be successful.

Dedication

People that have a desire to be great and who are willing to put in the hard work necessary to achieve their goals, can also be those people that are the most dedicated to your organization, if they feel that they are being treated fairly.

A person who is hard working and dedicated can be counted on to be constantly improving. They are not happy with the status quo and want to always get better. These are the "A-listers" and they're the people you need to surround yourself with. A dedicated employee is a happy employee that will go the extra mile. They are the type of people that truly want the company to succeed and have a "can-do" attitude. Unfortunately, these are also the people that your competitors want to steal from you so you must find a way to keep them involved and interested.

Dedicated employees are willing to help other team members who may be struggling, even as they work to get their own stuff done. They are the people who ask "what can I do to help" and don't sit back to rest as soon as their tasks have been completed. A dedicated person volunteers for things outside their typical duties because they know it will help the company and benefit the other members of their team.

One of the most extreme examples of dedication to their family and business comes from Dave Givens in Mariposa, CA as reported on www.theweek.com:

> *Unless you work from home, chances are you endure a less-than-pleasant commute. But none is likely as arduous as that of Dave Givens. The Mariposa, Calif., resident earned the unenviable award for "America's Longest Commute" when the muffler company Midas set out to find the employee who trekked the most miles to work.*
>
> *From his ranch home in Mariposa, Givens drives 186 miles to his job at Cisco Systems, Inc., in San Jose. The electrical engineer has been making this 372-mile round trip, which equals a total of seven hours of driving, for 17 years. "I have a great job and my family loves the ranch where we live," Givens said. "So this is the only solution." His dedication to the horrendous commute earned Givens the grand prize of $10,000 and some much-needed gas money as well as an array of Midas maintenance services and products.*

A truly dedicated employee like Givens is not always easy to find. They don't typically walk through the door with their dedication and commitment firmly entrenched. They may have an innate desire and understand the importance of dedication, but they need to see and feel each day that their commitment is being recognized and respected. If they feel that their dedication is one-sided their hard work will quickly dwindle.

Seek these people out, nurture them and show them that the dedication you get from them will be returned. You will not be disappointed!

Developing a good work ethic

There are a number of things that you can do, and that your teammates can do, in order to increase your work ethic. Please take note of the following ideas and see if they can have some value in your business life.

1. **Preparation** – Preparation is the key to success in anything that we do. If you know that you have a difficult task ahead then begin preparing whatever is necessary to succeed. Waiting until the last minute will only increase your frustration and minimize your chances of success. If you know you want to learn a new language then buy a book or software application on the topic BEFORE you begin taking the language class. This type of preparation makes everything easier and it will help you in the business world. Look to the future and prepare yourself for what may come along.

2. **Choose the hard things** – Begin your day by tackling the hardest tasks, not the easiest. For one thing, your energy level will be high in the morning and it might make it easier to accomplish your goals no matter how difficult they may be. Hard work is like a muscle, the more you do it the stronger you get. Attacking the hardest tasks first will makes it easier to go after the easier ones.

3. **Motivate yourself** - Identify what motivates you and figure out a way that additional hard work will help you attain that goal. You control your own motivation and having a positive mental attitude as you begin a difficult or arduous task will make it easier for you to tackle the problem and move on.

4. **Continuously challenge yourself** – Never be completely satisfied with your own performance. Obviously, you need to take pride in your accomplishments, but don't sit back on your laurels and expect your success to continue unless you push

yourself. You probably attained a level of success through hard work; and future success will most certainly be dependent upon you continuing to develop your work ethic.

5. **Continuously challenge your team members** – Push yourself, but also try and push your teammates in a healthy way. Create some internal competitions on who can complete their tasks in the quickest and most accurate fashion. Competition ALWAYS helps develop a solid work ethic.

6. **Commit to being the best** – Make a clear goal for yourself and then throw your efforts into making it happen. The more times that you can successfully do this the stronger your work ethic will be.

7. **Spend time on improving yourself** – Even if you feel overwhelmed at work, make sure to spend time on developing yourself. Everything starts with you and if you are not developing skills then your work performance will also soon begin to suffer.

Management Checklist

- ✓ Have I made a solid work ethic part of my daily life, or do I expect to turn it on and off as needed.
- ✓ Do I demonstrate my dedication to the company each day and is it clear to my team members?
- ✓ Do I truly know what my long term goals are and am I committed to achieving them?
- ✓ Do I have a burning desire to beat my competitors and to be the best leader that I can be?
- ✓ Do I discuss the benefits of hard work, a desire to be great, and dedication with my team in order to help them develop these attributes as well?

"I'm a greater believer in luck, and I find the harder I work the more I have of it" – **Thomas Jefferson**

"A dream doesn't become reality through magic; it takes sweat, determination and hard work." – **Colin Powell**

"Leaders aren't born they are made. And they are made just like anything else, through hard work. And that's the price we'll have to pay to achieve that goal, or any goal."– **Vince Lombardi**

Chapter 3 - Enthusiasm

Think about a time in your life when you were truly excited to do something, whether it was a visit to the zoo as a kid, a golf game at a beautiful resort course, or a romantic trip to the Caribbean. Think about the feelings you had leading up to the event. You were probably happy and filled with enthusiasm about what would happen next. This is the type of feeling that you want the people in your organization to express and feel as often as possible.

Have fun!

Many factors lead to enthusiasm at work and one of the most important is in creating a fun environment. Without some sort of fun you diminish enthusiasm, without enthusiasm you diminish motivation, and without motivation you greatly diminish your chance at long term business success.

Take a look at the following excerpt from the **Levity Effect: Why it Pays to Lighten Up**, by Adrian Gostick and Scott Christopher:

> *"...An excited Kirt Womack of the Thiokol factory in Utah sprinted into his manager's office on the first day of spring and asked if the folks on the factory floor could do something fun -- say, head outside and fly paper airplanes -- if they met their quota two hours early. The manager wrinkled his brow and vetoed the idea. Kirt persisted, "Well, then, what if we exceed our quota by 50 percent?" Figuring he had nothing to lose, the manager finally gave in.*
>
> *Later that day, at 1:30, the manager checked on things and found that his employees had reached 110 percent of their quota. By 3 p.m., they'd surpassed 150 percent.*

The airplanes were launched, laughter rang out and people frolicked (funny word, frolicked).

This tale is no big deal, right? Sure, except for the fact that a 50 percent increase isn't exactly insignificant. While this tale illustrates the benefits of levity at work, it also underscores the dire need to enlighten management. You should know what the supervisor's initial reaction was to his workers' hitting the 150 percent production goal by 3 p.m. Rather than connecting the dots and seeing the link between the promise of fun and working harder, he instead commented, "Imagine what you guys could have accomplished if you hadn't taken two hours off to screw around!"

The manager's initial ignorance did little to dissuade the workers. The kind of joyous, playful, break-the-tension fun they engaged in is taking place all around the world in organizations that care about performance, retention and profitability. Motivated purely by the opportunity to have a little fun at work, the aviation workers increased their performance dramatically. The next week they negotiated for a volleyball game on the factory floor as a reward and again hit record production levels. Each week, they continued to request fun rewards and turned in astounding production numbers. By the third week, when they had earned a trip offsite for ice cream cones, the manager finally got it.

It's hard to believe that a warm and fuzzy subject such as fun could impact an organization's success. But the remarkable case for levity at work is growing, with the most convincing numbers culled from more than a decade of research by the Great Place to Work Institute. Data from the organization's 1 million-person research database reveals that "Great" companies consistently earn significantly higher marks for "fun."

Each year, the Great Place to Work Institute asks tens of thousands of employees to rate their experience of workplace factors, including, "This is a fun place to work." On Fortune's "100 Best Companies to Work For" list, produced by the Great Place to Work Institute, employees in companies that are denoted as "great" responded overwhelmingly -- an average of 81 percent -- that they are working in a "fun" environment. That's a compelling statistic: Employees at the best companies are also having the best time. At the "good" companies -- those that apply for inclusion but do not make the top 100 -- only 62 employees out of 100 say they are having fun."

This is an amazing statistic, but sadly the message is too often overlooked at many organizations. I once worked for a company in which the Chief Financial Officer would scold his employees anytime he heard laughter from his team members *(if you can actually call them that)*. I also had an extremely boring summer job in which I sat in a hot warehouse and manually placed price tags on screwdrivers, pliers and other hardware items one at a time. A line of college students sitting at folding tables performed this unenviable task each day and we often carried on light hearted banter in order to make the time go by faster, and to make the task at hand a little more enjoyable. Unfortunately, our immediate supervisor did not share our desire to create a decent work environment when we were soon told to stop talking because we *"were there to work and not to have fun"*. Sadly this type of management philosophy was applied to the entire organization as it was the most stoic, drab work environment I have ever seen. No one seemed to have fun – ever. I never met an employee that cared about the company or that demonstrated a desire to put any in extra effort to help the company succeed. Within a few years this warehouse went out of business and although I have no hard core proof, I am quite sure a large portion of its demise was due to the poor work environment and the overall lack of enthusiasm from its employees.

It must be said, however, that having fun at work, as important as it is, is not the only thing that will help foster enthusiastic, motivated employees. Creating a team environment in which everyone feels that they are working toward a long term goal also works quite well. Acting with honesty and integrity is another solid way of developing enthusiasm in your workforce, and communicating to your team often and in a positive fashion will also help tremendously. All of these are covered thoroughly throughout this book and they dramatically affect the enthusiasm you will see demonstrated daily.

Business managers and owners are key contributors in helping to develop a fun and enthusiastic workforce, but as an employee you play a significant role as well. How many people report to work each day in a grumpy mood and perform their work without any enthusiasm? How many are there simply to pick up a paycheck? While there is certainly nothing wrong with working to put food on your table, why not try to find a job that excites you? Why not find a career that will enable you to be enthusiastic and happy in what you are doing every day?

Choose your attitude

Throughout my career, I have worked with a number of very talented and hard-working people that were absolutely terrible to be around. On paper they had most certainly experienced some success, but they did not enjoy what they were doing. It seemed that they were putting in the effort strictly so they could gain the experience and use it to find another job. At best, people like this will only be short term contributors and their lack of a positive attitude will actually begin to weigh down others within your organization. As an individual, you have the ability to control your situation and whether or not you will be miserable or enthusiastic.

There is an excellent book called **Fish** written by Stephen Lundin, Harry Paul, and John Christensen. Among other things, it details a business called the Pike Place Fish Market in Seattle and the benefits they receive through the daily enthusiasm displayed by their employees.

Apparently, the Pike Place Fish Market used to be a terrible place to work and was often referred to as a toxic energy dump until the team members discovered one amazing thing that can be applied to any business. *"There is always a choice about the way you do your work, even if there is not a choice about the work itself."* The authors of Fish refer to this as your ability to "choose your attitude" and this is an extremely valuable piece of advice.

In the book, the owner of the Pike Place Fish Market discusses his childhood, the lessons he learned, and the joy he received while washing dishes in the kitchen with his grandmother. He experienced these things, not because washing dishes was an enjoyable job, but because of the enthusiasm she brought to the task. By dispensing large amounts of love, wisdom and advice, she made the task of washing dishes fun for a young boy. This ultimately taught him that you could still have an enjoyable and productive time even if the thing you were doing was not enjoyable by itself.

This valuable lesson also became understood by the employees of the Pike Place Fish Market. They came to realize that when they showed up to work each day that they could bring an attitude with them, and it was the *kind of attitude* they brought that was the real issue! They could be moody, depressing, or grouchy; or they could bring a sunny, playful and cheerful attitude that would make customers happy and want to return. They soon realized that since they were going to be at work each day in a fish market that they might as well have the best possible day that they could, and it worked. The Pike Place Fish Market soon became famous for the crowds they drew on a daily basis... all to watch men and women having fun while at work in a fish market!

If a group of people can make working in a fish market fun and enthusiastic then I would imagine that most people working in a typical office environment can also find a way to do the same thing. Not only will it help you as an employee reach a level of satisfaction each day, but it will make you more attractive to prospective employers.

Why enthusiasm is important

The US Department of Labor published some interesting information on the importance business manager's place on enthusiasm in the workforce:

> *"When employers look at prospective candidates, beyond skills, experience, and training, they look for those who demonstrate enthusiasm – those they believe will complete assigned tasks in an upbeat and cooperative manner.*
>
> *All other things being equal, a candidate who can demonstrate a positive attitude and eagerness to tackle the job will have an advantage over one who displays an attitude viewed by the employer as negative or disinterested. In fact, many employers would rather provide job skills training to an enthusiastic but inexperienced worker than hire someone with perfect qualifications but a less-than-positive attitude. Managers sometimes worry that this type of person will not get along with supervisors and co-workers, treat customers disrespectfully, and not put much effort into his or her work. On the other hand, employees who are viewed as enthusiastic are known to provide good customer service, resolve interpersonal conflict effectively, and work productively with others.*

There are many ways in which an individual might demonstrate enthusiasm in the workplace. For example, in a job interview, he or she might smile, sit up straight, make eye contact, and discuss training and work experiences in an upbeat manner.

Once hired into a position, an enthusiastic employee will typically show up on time, show interest in his or her job, and demonstrate a willingness to listen, learn, and try new things. In customer service settings, an enthusiastic employee will approach customers proactively and offer assistance or seek out tasks and projects when there is down time. This positive attitude helps employees go above and beyond to get along with co-workers and managers – even difficult ones – and respond to constructive criticism with maturity and willingness to improve.

Overall, an employee with enthusiasm comes across as someone who wants to be at work and who is willing to do what it takes to get the job done."

I doubt that many people who have been in leadership roles would argue with any of the statements above. I agree 100% with the sentiments, especially as it relates to hiring someone who clearly displays a high level of enthusiasm.

If you do this on an on-going basis, you probably will achieve more and hopefully earn more money throughout your career. More importantly, an enthusiastic attitude will lift people up and attract other people of a like mind to join your organization. Pretty soon your enthusiasm will infect those around you and your entire company will be seeking out new and better ideas on how to do things and complete projects in more imaginative ways. Enthusiasm can (and should) be a core aspect of a company culture. It also means that people will enjoy coming to work and that they will be less likely to seek a position elsewhere.

Motivational keynote speaker, Jody Urquhart published lovely great article on creating a fun workplace that is so on point that I have included it nearly verbatim:

> **There are 3 ways to motivate people to work harder, faster and smarter:**
>
> > *1. Threaten them.*
> > *2. Pay them lots of money.*
> > *3. Make their work fun.*
>
> *In today's workplace, threatening people has not been effective. Paying them lots of money (even if you can afford it) has only shown short-term success. Only number three, making their workplace enjoyable, has a track record of effecting real change. It is time managers learned how to create an atmosphere that is challenging, creative and fun for employees as well as for themselves.*
>
> ### HOW FUN IS PRODUCTIVE
>
> *Imagine a work world where people love their work environment, and they are calm, stress-free and happy all day long. People who are in good spirits are more likely to be productive. Their mental attitude produces increased oxygen, endorphins, and blood flow to the brain, which enables them to think more clearly and creatively. They are more relaxed, more accepting of others, and more likely to share their sense of humor.*
>
> *Laughter creates a bond that brings others together; people like to be with employees who are having fun. Creativity, intuition and flexibility are key to successful*

operation of organizations today. In stimulating environments, employees enjoy their time at work and they will also excel at work. Attracting customers is easier in an environment of hospitality. A fun workplace is not only more productive, but it attracts people and profits.

A TEST: IS YOUR STAFF SUFFERING FROM TERMINAL SERIOUSNESS?

Scan your workplace and take note:

- *Do you regularly catch people laughing or smiling at work?*
- *When something funny happens do people stop and appreciate it?*
- *Does your organization have fun activities at least monthly?*
- *Do you have tools (fun giveaways, drawings) to invite employees to participate in having fun in your environment?*
- *Are managers usually optimistic and smiling at work?*

If you answer "no" to two or more of these questions then your staff probably suffers from "terminal seriousness," which is negatively affecting morale and productivity.

More Benefits of Humor in the Workplace

Dr. Norman Cousins said, "Laughter is an igniter of great expectations." Children laugh an average of 400 times a day and that number drops to only 15 times a day by the time people reach age 35. Preschoolers must know something we don't. Laughter releases endorphins (a chemical 10 times more powerful than the pain-relieving drug morphine) into the body with the same exhilarating effect as doing strenuous exercise. Laughing increases oxygen intake, thereby replenishing and invigorating cells. It also increases the pain threshold, boosts immunity, and relieves stress.

Humor also levels the playing field to create an atmosphere that encourages honest dialogue, open communication, and increased risk-taking. Creating more equality in power or control shows people respect and builds pride in their work.

This is just a sampling of the benefits of having fun in your workplace. Hopefully now you are convinced you could use a "fun injection" in your own place of employment.

Help people belong to your organization and not just work there by giving them a way to solidify and build rapport.

THIRTEEN STEPS TO CREATING A FUN WORKPLACE:

1. Give up the notion that professionalism means being serious all the time - It's possible to take yourself lightly and still be competent and productive. Start to promote the benefits of humor at work.

2. Define what fun is in your workplace and what it is not - e.g. harmful humor, off-color jokes, sexual humor, humor tarnishing the organization

3. Organize a "Fun Committee" for dreaming up fun "stuff" to do during and after work – Let your staff come up with new ideas to keep things interesting!

4. Add fun to meetings - *Bring in fun things such as Nerf balls, a basketball and hoop, or party blowers. Start a meeting with a humorous story or joke.*

5. Collect and share your favorite cartoons and jokes - *Create a Joke Board or a Humor Newsletter. Look for tools to disseminate fun and funny things daily.*

6. Let customers know you are a fun company - *Do something just for fun (organize fun customer events, dress for fun, share funny things with customers) and give employees tools to create a fun relationship with customers (stickers, candy for children, dog biscuits for dogs, humorous buttons with the company logo). This makes work more fun for employees and it strengthens the relationship with customers. Dick Snow of Ben and Jerry's Ice Cream says, "We believe that we're in the entertainment business and selling ice cream is just a part of what we do. In our stores the counter is our stage and the customers are our audience." Disneyland has the same kind of approach. Employees are part of an entertainment experience, and they aren't just doing a job.*

7. Gather your co-workers for the "Joy of Work" hour - *Everyone must talk about something good at work. Take turns telling stories about the things that make work a joy. Each person should contribute ideas on how to make work more fun.*

8. Have a fun recognition program - *Fun is not a reward for performance, but can be a way to encourage employees to perform. For example, you could create "games" out of productive activity...who can motivate the most patients in a hospital to smile and say something funny to the head nurse. Playful and goal-oriented fun is best.*

9. Respond to fun when it happens - *Funny things occur all the time, but if you are obsessed with left-brain analytical thought, you might find it hard to stop and respond. Natural spontaneous humor is a blessing. Stop and take a moment to give employees and customers an opportunity to see the fun in the event.*

10. Commit to being fun and it will change your approach to work - *Start slowly with a few activities and communicate your desire to create a more relaxed workplace. Don't expect things to turn around overnight.*

11. Put fun things and activities in the staff room - *This allows people to take their mind off of the seriousness of work for a short period, so they come back to work with a more positive and balanced perspective.*

12. Encourage staff to leave work behind at the end of the day - *Employees shouldn't be so consumed with work that it affects their family life and leisure activities. Find fun ways for employees to "unload" at the end of the day or week. Create a ritual like writing a "to do" list and posting it on the board. By doing this, you commit to not thinking about the things on the list until the next day.*

13. Encourage employees to develop their own style of having fun - *A nurse anesthetist at a hospital in Michigan often sings to his patients to help them relax prior to surgery. Patients have appreciated this so much that they have told family and friends about the experience. It is not uncommon now for the hospital staff to get requests for "The Singing Anesthesiologist" when they are scheduling their surgery.*

Fun and enthusiasm at work

One of the more successful organizations around right now is Google, and they have led the "fun" revolution for a number of years. Although I've never visited their headquarters, it's reported that employees climb ladders between floors, race around the building on scooters and design their own workspace with handwriting on the walls and the occasional treadmill strategically placed throughout the office. According to Jordan Newman, Manager, Corporate Communications and Public Affairs at Google their offices around the globe are designed to reflect the company's overall philosophy which is "to create the happiest, most productive workplace in the world." It must be working because over the past 12 months their stock has risen by over 25% which is more than twice that of the Dow Jones Industrial Averages.

It is imperative to the development of a successful business that you find people that bring enthusiasm to the table each day. The people with a "can-do" attitude that want to show the world what can be done. Enthusiasm is infectious and it can change the entire dynamic of a group in very positive ways. I believe that you want people who are excited to come to work each day and not those who find it a chore. The people that lack enthusiasm will most often be an average contributor at best. Don't hire these people. If a person lacks enthusiasm and interest in an interview imagine how they will be once they actually have the job.

Many people have an inherent enthusiasm about them when they join an organization, but a truly successful business person must continue to nurture this or it will fade. It's important to continually do things with your team that will make their day enjoyable and keep them interested and enthusiastic. Thank people often and let them see how much they are appreciated. It only takes a few seconds to recognize someone for a job well done. You will be surprised at how much good will this creates, especially if it is done in front of their colleagues. Make their work experience as fun and enjoyable as possible and always let them know that you want them to be happy. There are 24 hours in a day. Eight of them are spent sleeping, another eight at home with family and friends and the last eight are spent at work. This means that nearly 50% of your waking hours are spent at work. Why not develop a workplace that fosters enthusiasm and fun?

Don't be afraid. People will be happier to show up to work each day and I guarantee their performance and results will improve!

Management Checklist:

   ✓   Do I truly believe that happy enthusiastic people will make my business stronger?
   ✓   Do I display enthusiasm on a daily basis that others can readily see?
   ✓   Do I help foster an enthusiastic workforce by taking part in interesting activities with my team members?
   ✓   Do I communicate to everyone in the organization that it is ok to have fun?
   ✓   When hiring a new employee, do I seek people out that clearly demonstrate enthusiasm during the interview process?

"None are so old as those who have outlived enthusiasm." - **Henry David Thoreau**

"Enthusiasm spells the difference between mediocrity and accomplishment." – **Norman Vincent Peale**

"With an enthusiastic team you can achieve almost anything." – **Tahir Shah**

Chapter 4 - Resilience

The Merriam-Webster Dictionary defines resilience as *"an ability to recover from or adjust easily to misfortune or change".*

We all know that life is not always easy. Dealing with change or loss is an inevitable part of our journey and we will all experience certain setbacks at work and on a personal basis. Some of these challenges will be minor, while others will affect us on a much larger scale. How we handle these situations from an emotional and psychological standpoint plays a significant role in how things ultimately turn out.

During the course of our lives we may have witnessed some people who seem to remain calm when faced with a difficult or disastrous situation, while others seem to panic and fall apart. We may have wondered how these people are able to keep their cool during great times of stress and display what psychologists typically refer to as resilience, or an ability to handle problems and setbacks in an appropriate and professional manner. Resilient people are able to utilize their skill, background and emotional fortitude to recover from what others might deem to be monumental problems and challenges, like unemployment, bankruptcy, divorce, or the loss of a loved one.

People who lack this type of psychological resilience often times become overwhelmed by these experiences. Some become nearly paralyzed by the problems they face and may use unhealthy coping mechanisms such as drugs and alcohol to deal with their challenges. Generally, these individuals do not recover as quickly from setbacks and may experience a great deal of long term psychological distress.

Being resilient does not eliminate bad things from happening, but it does provide the internal strength to deal with negative situations in an appropriate fashion, and to ultimately move on with their lives or business.

Resilience develops throughout your life as you gain knowledge and self-management and positive coping skills. It's also greatly influence by how you were raised and the support you received from your parents, family and peers. It can certainly be strengthened over time, but if your early childhood did nothing to prepare you for the inevitable hardships we will all face, then it will be difficult to develop this skill as an adult.

Examples of resilience

Many well recognized business people have experienced horrific failures and setbacks but ultimately prevailed. Obviously, these individuals all exhibited a high level of resilience:

Henry Ford – Failed in early business and went bankrupt five times before he achieved success with the Ford Motor Company.

Walt Disney – Was bankrupt at one point in his career and was fired from one position because he lacked imagination and had no good ideas!

Colonel Sanders – Famed for his success with Kentucky Fried Chicken, he tried to sell his secret recipe to over 1,000 restaurants before it was finally accepted.

Soichiro Honda – Was rejected for an engineering position at Toyota. Without a job he started making scooters at home that he sold to his neighbors. After getting financial support from his family, he founded Honda, one of the world's most profitable and well respected automobile manufacturers.

Winston Churchill - One of the most famous examples of true resilience can be illustrated by reviewing what happened to Winston Churchill during WWI and the failed battle now referred to simply as Gallipoli. In 1915 Churchill was a 40 year old First

Lord of the Admiralty, and Germany was making great advances against the western allies. Considering himself a master strategist, Churchill pushed for a land and sea invasion on a Northwest peninsula of Turkey called Gallipoli and the Dardanelles Strait with the hopes of opening up a supply route to their Russian Allies. His plan would provide Russia with grain and military supplies to strengthen a second front against the enemy. Although everyone realized the risks involved, the overall campaign failed miserably. Countless articles have been written as to all of the causes, but Churchill, given his lead role in the planning, bore the brunt of the blame and later that year he was demoted to an obscure cabinet post.

According to Christopher Klein in his article entitled Winston Churchill's World War Disaster he states the following about Churchill's attitude and resilience:

> *"I am the victim of a political intrigue," he lamented to a friend. "I am finished!" Displaying the steely determination that would serve him well in World War II, however, the marginalized Churchill did not slink from the fight. In November 1915, the statesman turned soldier. Churchill resigned from the government, picked up a gun and headed to the front lines in France as an infantry officer with the Royal Scots Fusiliers. After several brushes with death, he returned to politics in 1917 as the munitions minister in a new coalition government headed by Liberal Prime Minister David Lloyd George.*

> *Churchill, however, remained haunted by Gallipoli for decades. "Remember the Dardanelles," his political opponents taunted when he stood up to speak in the House of Commons. When running for Parliament in 1923, hecklers called out, "What about the Dardanelles?" The "British Bulldog" embraced Gallipoli as a brilliant failure. "The Dardanelles might have saved*

millions of lives. Don't imagine I am running away from the Dardanelles. I glory in it," he responded.

Although many shared the views of a political insider who in 1931 speculated that "the ghosts of Gallipoli will always rise up to damn him anew," Churchill became prime minister in 1940 with Britain once again embroiled in war. Upon taking office, he wrote, "All my past life had been a preparation for this hour and for this trial." That included Gallipoli.

What an amazing story of resilience in what many consider to be one of the greatest leaders of the 20th Century. Few doubt that his will and tenacity played a significant role in the Battle of Britain and ultimately in the allies victory during WWII. Without his tremendous resilience our world would most likely be a vastly different place.

Lack of resilience

Unfortunately, many people in the business world are ill equipped to deal with setbacks or even minor changes within an organization. Perhaps it comes from a lack of confidence or how they were brought up, but my 30 years of experience in business has proven to me that truly resilient people are hard to find. Just look at the success of a book like **Who Moved My Cheese**, which was written to help people adapt and deal with the inevitable change that takes place in virtually every organization. Obviously, 26 million copies would not have been sold if a large segment of the population was already imbued with a true sense of resilience.

What are some of the overwhelming concerns of people who lack resilience?

- **Loss of control** – No one wants to feel that they have lost control over a situation. Those with resilience will take time to stop and rationally examine a situation.

They will then create a plan in order to rectify things and get back on track. It is this type of mental planning and strategizing that makes people with resilience seem to handle stressful situations better than most.

- **Excess uncertainty** – In the business world there is always a lot of uncertainty. No one has all of the answers because if they did we would not have had failed products such as New Coke, Colgate Kitchen Entrees, or the Apple Newton. Many people think that if big organizations can make such huge mistakes, how can my manager at our small business possibly get it right?

- **The surprise factor** – Often times, employees are not privy to everything that is going on behind the scenes and are caught off guard when catastrophe hits; and if changes are required to their business.

- **It's too different** – Many people become creatures of habit and when their routine needs to change they become uncomfortable.

- **Loss of face** – Change is a departure from the past and those people who were leaders under the old way of doing things may be resentful and fear that they will be viewed harshly by those around them. It takes a strong person to be able to admit when they were wrong and to figure out the best way forward.

- **Can I do it?** - Over time people become familiar with how things are done on a day to day basis. If that is scheduled to change some of these people will doubt whether or not they can actually perform as well as they had in the past. From my experience, most people can actually adapt quite well to most change. It is whether or not they want to that is the real question.

- **Waiting for the other shoe to drop** – Is this the first of many changes? What is wrong with the way we were doing things? *What will happen next? What will happen next? What will happen next?*

- **Past changes** – "I have been here for 20 years and I have seen all kinds of different changes....none of them ever work and this is going to be a failure as well".

These feelings are very normal and prevalent for many people in the working world. This is especially true given the uncertainty in the US economy over the past few years. As a leader, it is your job to show your resilience daily. You must demonstrate a positive attitude at all times because your team members will look to you when things get tough. If they see a worried, concerned person then they too will become worried and concerned. But if they see a strong figure that confidently maps a new way forward they will feel much more comfortable with what is going on around them. Over time, your team will begin to handle issues in a healthier fashion if you can act as their guide.

I had a friend that worked for a company based out of Sweden that had recently been bought by a publicly traded company from the US. Experiencing the attitude of the hard driving "Americans" with a total focus on the bottom line was somewhat of a shock to the Swedes. Even though the company had been profitable in the past, it was no longer enough and the new owners were insisting on a major overhaul. She told me that half of the executive management team were convinced that the changes being demanded would drive the company out of business, and the other half were preparing themselves for quitting or getting fired. In other words there was a lot of panic going on within the management team.

At one budget meeting the CEO of the publicly traded company slammed his hand on the table and told them that he would not accept the figures they had presented and abruptly ended the meeting. He told the entire worldwide executive management team that they had until the next morning to revise the numbers or else. Needless to say there was a lot of hand wringing and worried people when the management team convened in a separate room to re-work the budget. My friend described some people as being in "a state of total paralysis". Many people in the room simply sat in silence and seemed overwhelmed by what had just happened.

Apparently, the Swedish business manager was so lost that her lone suggestion was to recommend spending over $1 million dollars on consultants who would then in turn tell them what to do. Luckily, my friend has a high level of resilience and was able to calm the team down, get them focused, and ultimately convinced them that they could accomplish what many people in the room felt was a total impossibility. Over many hours and a lot of tough decisions a new plan was devised which satisfied the new owners. Presenting a plan to spend exorbitant amounts on outside consultants would have been disastrous for the entire team and it was a strong team member with a high level of resilience that was able to save the day.

These are the types of people you need to add to your team. You want people that may have previously faced setbacks and failure, but who have also persevered. They will add a certain level of toughness to your organization that will help you through the inevitable rough patches. They will not give up easily and will continue to search for solutions.

How to be more resilient

Jessica Kleiman published a list in *Forbes*, of seven things to help you bounce back from a bad situation:

1. **Hope for the Best, Prepare for the Worst**
   - *Go with your gut.* When you see a red flag, pay attention. How many times in life have you kicked yourself for not listening to that little voice in your head that says, "Something is wrong here"?
   - *Have a plan and a back-up plan.* Try to lay out a strategy and do our best to identify potential pitfalls and problems on the horizon. While we may not always be able to predict what's coming our way, by doing the exercise and putting a solid plan on paper,

you'll be prepared to deal with it if the issue ever sees the light of the day.

2. Be a Problem Solver

- *Stay calm.* In a crisis, people tend to get anxious. Maintaining a sense of Zen will not only allow you to think more clearly but will also set the tone for those around you.
- *Get focused.* You want to quickly assess the damage and determine how to move forward.
- *Find a solution.* Next, you need to figure out how to address and remedy the situation. Start by considering your end game — what's the ultimate outcome you'd like to see? — And work backwards from there.

3. Own up

- *Take responsibility.* If you screwed up, don't make excuses — just apologize for any misstep, miscommunication or oversight on your part.
- *Be authentic.* People can tell whether you mean what you say. JetBlue cancelled 1,000 flights in 2007 when an ice storm crippled its operations. Instead of blaming the weather, then CEO David Neeleman made a public apology detailing what they would do to make it right with their customers. Ultimately, it resulted in a customer bill of rights that clearly spells out what the company will do in case of future service interruptions.

4. Control the Damage, Clean Up the Mess

- *Act quickly.* Don't let a small mistake linger and turn into a bigger one. That's not to say you should simply be reactive, but if you know you did something wrong, deal with it right away. Say, for example, you stuck your foot in your mouth during an important business meeting and inadvertently offended your boss or a client. Acknowledge the gaffe, apologize and try to move on without beating yourself up. Remember what Theodore

Roosevelt once said, "In any moment of decision, the best thing you can do is the right thing, the next thing is the wrong thing, and the worst thing you can do is nothing."

5. **Keep Things in Perspective**

- *Learn and let it go.* Often when we mess up, we tend to be hard on ourselves or over analyze an error, reliving the mistake over and over. But rarely will the crises we deal with be life or death so it's important to be able to step back and take a 10,000 foot view of the situation and its long-term effects.
- *Everybody loves a comeback.* In most cases, if you fix a problem quickly and show that you can move past it, others will be able to as well. Our society likes nothing more than a survivor story (see Martha Stewart, Charlie Sheen, Robert Downey, Jr., etc.), so respond smartly and swiftly so that you can recover.

6. **Turn Trouble into Triumph**

- Make that lemonade: When you're going through (or almost on the other side of) a crisis, look for the silver lining. Get into an argument with someone? Perhaps it opened up a new dialogue that wasn't previously possible. Did you stumble and fall (either literally or figuratively)? Learn to laugh at yourself, find the humor or lesson in whatever the situation.

7. **Fail Forward**

- *Find the lesson.* My favorite interview question is "Tell me about a time when you failed, how you dealt with it, and what you learned." The answer will broadcast how someone handles a crisis and whether the experience made him or her more effective at work or in life.
- *Join the club.* Nearly every successful person – from Steve Jobs to NYC Mayor Michael Bloomberg to Oprah Winfrey – has been fired from a job. Nearly every inventor has failed at something

before they made it big. For example, a scientist at 3M was attempting to develop a super-strong adhesive but instead created weak glue that didn't leave residue. Because his experiment failed, his error led to one of the most successful inventions ever (who doesn't love a Post-it?).

- *Lead by example.* What you learn from failure helps you identify new ways of doing things and allows you to grow and become a better manager and leader.

One of your most important characteristics as a manager needs to be your resilience in dealing with the inevitable, every day issues that are faced by every business AND the one-off crisis situations that can cripple an organization if not handled correctly. If you're resilient and handle things correctly, then your people will begin to show resilience as well. Finding, keeping and developing strong, resilient people will help your organization be successful.

Management Checklist

- ✓ Do I handle difficult situations in a calm, professional manner on a day-to-day basis?
- ✓ Do I communicate frequently to my team to keep them abreast of potential changes within the organization?
- ✓ Do I provide adequate training to people when I expect them to perform a new task or do I contribute to their uneasiness by assuming that they can perform to expectations?
- ✓ Do I listen to my team and help to address their needs and concerns when brought to my attention?
- ✓ Do I recognize the signs of stress within myself and my team members?

"I have not failed. I've just found 10,000 ways that won't work." — **Thomas Edison**

"Success is not final, failure is not fatal: it is the courage to continue that counts." – **Winston Churchill**

"You may encounter many defeats, but you must not be defeated. In fact, it may be necessary to encounter the defeats, so you can know who you are, what you can rise from, how you can still come out of it." – **Maya Angelou**

Chapter 5 - Personal Accountability

My father was a sergeant in the Marines during World War II and was stationed in the South Pacific for most of his tour of duty. After his return to the good old US of A he drove a local delivery truck for the next thirty years, never making more than $22,000 a year. He was brought up during the hard scrabble days of the depression and joined the military service right out of high school. As you might imagine, he was a tough, no nonsense guy and frankly not always the easiest person to deal with. Regardless of the situation he taught me many valuable things, one of which was to take personal responsibility for my actions. It was, and is, one of the most valuable pieces of wisdom I have ever received. I remember his talks in which he explained how everyone would be faced with a lot of different choices during their lifetime and that it was important for each of us to evaluate them, their consequences, and to ultimately make the right decision. He especially stressed that I really think about the impact that my choices would have upon not just my life; but how my actions might affect other members of my family or people that we cared about.

This stuck with me and over the years it became even more meaningful to me as I matured. Have I always been perfect in applying this theory? Absolutely not, but it is one of the major reasons that I have been successful in my business career and why I have been able to do the right thing more often than not. His words often echoed in my head that my actions would define me, and that it would be my actions that would determine whether or not I was successful. No one else was going to do it for me!

A lack of accountability

Without wanting to sound too curmudgeonly, I think that this type of personal responsibility has somehow gotten lost along the way. I don't have any statistics or studies to cite, but my gut tells me that many people today seem to have a certain level of entitlement based upon nothing more than the fact that they are alive. It appears to me that not many people adopt the attitude that they need to control their destiny, that they can greatly influence their success, or that they have any personal responsibility for their overall actions. As I write this, *"the devil made me do it"* as a cynical, yet humorous way to avoid personal responsibility continually pops into my mind!

Linda Adams, President of Gordon Training International sums up the lack of personal responsibility in our society quite nicely on the GTI webpage:

> *"There's nothing I can do."*
> *"It's up to him/her."*
> *"I had a dysfunctional childhood."*
> *"I never get a break."*
> *"I can't do that because…"*
> *"I'm so unlucky."*
>
> *Many of us live as though someone or something outside of ourselves controls our lives. Whether it be other people, our parents, background, age, sex, race, fear, fate or God, we behave as if we are not active agents who are responsible for ourselves.*
>
> *We wait.*
>
> *We wait for something to happen or someone to come along to fulfill our needs or to make our lives better. But as the self-esteem author, Nathaniel Branden expressed it so aptly, "No one is coming."*

That's right. No one is coming!

Success is up to you

It's up to you to be successful. I firmly believe that when you take individual and personal responsibility for your actions that your overall performance will improve, that you will become a model for others to follow, and that your success in the business world will increase. It doesn't mean that you won't make mistakes, but taking responsibility for those mistakes will hopefully allow you to learn something and become a better person and leader.

I have often heard sales people complain that the products they had been asked to sell were too expensive, that the services offered to the customer after the sale were not good enough, or that certain competitors were stealing business from them. These were just a few of the reasons why they were not being successful in sales. Granted these can certainly be viable reasons, but the rationale soon fell apart when other people in the organization selling the same products, offering the same after sales service, and facing the same competitors met with a tremendous amount of success. It is amazing that two people can look at virtually an identical scenario and one will become a victim while another will thrive.

The difference is that the successful sales person decided that they were going to take personal responsibility for their success and not dwell on the negative situations that every organization must certainly have. They made a decision that they were going to be successful and devised a plan to achieve that success. They were not going to let the typical issues outside of their control have a negative effect upon their ability to succeed. This is the meaning of taking personal responsibility for your actions.

Tom Herman and Associates posts this on their website about personal accountability:

> *"People that accept personal accountability take ownership of situations that they are involved in. They*

see them through, and ultimately take responsibility for the outcome whether or not things turn out good or bad. They certainly don't blame others if things go wrong and they always do their best to make things right."

I couldn't have said it better myself.

As a business manager it is imperative that you take this to heart and build it into your daily life.

Developing personal accountability

Ruben Navarrette published a column in which he lists the following suggestions for parents trying to teach personal responsibility to their children:

- *"Work hard, and teach your children to take summer and after school jobs. Don't treat any kind of work as beneath you. Someone has to do it, and you're no better than they are.*
- *Don't play the victim. Just because you didn't get a promotion doesn't mean you can duck responsibility by blaming affirmative action or other forces beyond your control.*
- *Raise your kids to be confident, but not narcissistic. Our youth are intoxicated with cheap self-esteem, taught to believe that everyone in a race deserves a trophy just for showing up.*
- *Don't think of yourself as entitled to anything. Don't worry about what you think you deserve. Just concentrate on doing what is necessary to earn what you want."*

This is great advice for people raising children. It certainly has benefits to those people reading this chapter that fall into this category, but I also firmly believe that it can be of service when coaching your employees on the importance of personal accountability. Why not talk to your team members about not being a victim and about being honest with what is going on around them? No harm can come of it and it may actually cause people to begin taking responsibility for their actions.

There are few other things you may want to consider as you develop your own skills in this area and during your coaching sessions with your teammates:

1. **Understand your role** - Become an expert in what you do and in the role you play within your organization. Having a clear understanding of your responsibilities will give you the confidence to know if you are doing things correctly, making the right decisions and planning the most impactful future activities.

2. **Be organized and manage your time** – Removing the obstacles to success that you can control will give you more time to focus on the important tasks at hand, and not searching for an important piece of paper or missing a deadline. The fewer simple mistakes you make because you are organized and manage your time wisely will increase your likelihood of success and again give you confidence to take on new tasks in a successful fashion.

3. **Don't take on too much** – Great employees are often sought out for new assignments because they are known to get things done accurately and on a timely basis. Unfortunately, these people can quickly become overloaded and it is important for them to communicate to their supervisor that the workload is becoming too much. The thing to remember is not to commit to a task if you cannot complete it as expected.

4. **Seek Assistance** – Despite your best efforts and planning you may become swamped and run behind on a project, but don't be afraid to ask for help. I do not know any decent manager that will find fault with this scenario. Most managers will want to know what they can do to help you achieve your goals; especially if they

know that you are organized and can manage your time wisely.

People that demonstrate personal accountability always achieve more in group setting because other team members realize that they are dependable and get things done on time. This also typically leads to more promotions and long term business success.

Visioncorp, a management consulting firm published the following information on their website that may be useful:

WAYS TO HOLD YOURSELF ACCOUNTABLE

1. *Focus on finding solutions for the problem, not on excuses*
2. *As a team or group leader, be willing to accept blame, even if the fault is not directly your own. Don't throw teammates or co-workers "under the bus".*
3. *Recognize how, even in a small way, you may have contributed to the problem.*
4. *In any problem situation, look at ways you might have handled things differently.*
5. *Let go of your concern about what others say or think about you.*
6. *Always strive to make those around you look good at their work.*
7. *Control your anger or any personal dislikes you may have for another.*
8. *Be honest in your own assessment of your strengths and weaknesses and be willing to share them with your colleagues.*
9. *Get comfortable with the phrase "I am sorry".*
10. *Get comfortable with the phrase "I was wrong"*

Make no mistake about it. You cannot achieve any worthwhile personal or professional goal if you don't hold yourself accountable. If you don't hold yourself accountable at work, don't expect to be promoted or to experience any type of significant career advancement. If you don't hold yourself accountable in your personal life with your parents, roommate or spouse, it will grow old fast and your relationships will deteriorate.

Examples of personal accountability

A great example of accepting personal responsibility comes to us from Greg Schiano, the ex-head coach of the Tampa Bay Buccaneers who had recently been fired from his position. In a statement to the press a few hours later he handled the situation with class and full personal responsibility. An article from the local news channel, WFLA and posted on their website recounted the story in the following way:

> *"Schiano was let go after two losing years extended the franchise's playoff drought to six seasons. General Manager Mark Dominik was also ousted, ending an unsuccessful five-year stint that produced flashes of hope but far more disappointment than ownership felt was acceptable.*
>
> *Schiano held a news conference Monday afternoon and reflected on his time with the Buccaneers.*
>
> *"It was quite an honor. I enjoyed every day of it," he said.*
>
> *"We didn't get it done. I accept full responsibility for that," said Schiano. "We didn't win enough games."*

That is personal responsibility. Not once did he claim that he didn't have the right players, that he got bad breaks from the referees, or that the *"sun was in his eyes"*. He understood that he was the head coach and that he alone was responsible for putting a winning team on the field. Granted, he could not actually control all of the members of his team and how they performed on an individual basis, but he did not blame anyone else for their lack of success. Although he lost his job, this type of personal responsibility will no doubt make him more appealing to someone else thinking about hiring him in the future. If he had whined about all of the bad breaks or poor players that he had I doubt that people will seriously consider him for a head coaching position sometime down the road. His personal responsibility will make him more attractive even though he wasn't successful during his stint at Tampa Bay.

Another example of personal responsibility can be found when examining the CEO of Netflix. Not too long ago the DVD rental service updated its pricing structure and obviously underestimated the impact it would have upon their customers and ultimately their business. CNN published this report online to illustrate how the Netflix CEO handled the situation:

> Netflix Co-founder and CEO Reed Hastings made a public apology in his blog on Sunday after a customer outburst against a hike in prices.
>
> "I messed up," Hastings said. "I owe everyone an explanation."
>
> Hastings posted the mea culpa after a barrage of customer backlash that caused Netflix stock to plunge.
>
> Netflix subscribers quit the service in droves last week after the unexpected increase. Enraged customers flooded the Netflix site with tens of thousands of comments, as well as a barrage of tweets under the hashtag #DearNetflix.
>
> "In hindsight, I slid into arrogance based upon past success," Hastings said. "We have done very well for a

long time by steadily improving our service, without doing much CEO communication."

Hastings goes on to explain the company's plans to rename its DVD-by-mail service Qwikster, while keeping the Netflix name for the online movie streaming service. Hastings also assures customers the price hike is over. "There are no pricing changes (we're done with that!)."

...Hastings closes the blog with another apology and the companies' commitment to "work hard to regain your trust. We know it will not be overnight. Actions speak louder than words. But words help people to understand actions."

Did Mr. Hastings actions work? I am not 100% certain, but soon after they made their pricing mistake, the Netflix stock had plummeted to approximately $67 a share. Within the next two plus years the stock had regained its' momentum and climbed to an all-time high of over $450. Was this precipitous rise strictly because of his mea culpa? I doubt it, but I guarantee that it helped!

Accepting personal responsibility for your actions is a key to your long term success. If you as a manager/owner make a mistake, admit it! There's nothing wrong with facing the fact that a decision you might have made did not turn out as expected and in identifying a new alternative. If you've been treating your employees fairly and been in constant communication with them then they'll probably have a lot of empathy with what happened and actually pull harder for you to succeed.

EVERYONE has made mistakes along the way. Admitting your mistakes to your teammates will let them know that it is ok as long as they were making a sincere, legitimate effort and that they acted with integrity along the way. The key is to admit that it was a mistake and determine a new, best path on which to continue. Dwelling on the past does nothing but increase anxiety, but you must also learn from these situations. Continuing to make the same mistakes over and over again without gaining knowledge is nothing but a waste of time, and the first step in destroying your business. Accept that a mistake has been made, but more importantly LEARN what caused it and how to avoid it in the future!

If one of your teammates makes a mistake, don't ridicule them. Work with them, help them identify and recognize the mistake and act as a leader to help map a new course of action. By doing this, the trust being built between you and your teammates will continue to develop and the likelihood of long term success will increase.

As a business owner or manager, finding people that have this characteristic will not always be easy as it has seemingly been an overlooked attribute over the past 15 to 20 years. Don't give up. They are out there. You just need to find them, nurture them, and build your business around them.

Management Checklist

- ✓ Do I readily admit to myself and my teammates when I have made a mistake or do I look for a scapegoat or create an excuse as to why something did not get completed as expected?
- ✓ Do I lose patience with my teammates when they come to me for help or if they admit that they have made a mistake?
- ✓ Do I encourage my teammates to be open and honest with each other and to take responsibility for the success of their teams?
- ✓ Do I spend time during my interview process trying to uncover the level of personal accountability demonstrated by each candidate under consideration?
- ✓ Have I done everything I can to develop a mindset of personal accountability within my team?

"You cannot escape the responsibility of tomorrow by evading it today." – **Abraham Lincoln**

"If you take responsibility for yourself you will develop a hunger to accomplish your dreams." – **Less Brown**

"We are made wise not by the recollection of our past, but by the responsibility for our future. " – **George Bernard Shaw**

Important Note

Now would be a good time for you to stop and review The Pyramid of Business Success illustration again. The five attributes that make up the base of our pyramid - Integrity, Hard Work, Enthusiasm, Resilience and Personal Accountability – are the foundation for a very specific reason. For the most part, these attributes are ingrained in people from a very early age. Someone who lacks integrity and who has been dishonest all their life is probably not going to all of a sudden become an "Honest Abe".

If they do not reach your organization with a desire and willingness to work hard then you will probably not be able to instill it in them. The same goes for the other three attributes at the base of my pyramid. People will either have these characteristics or they won't.

Granted some of these attributes can be honed and sharpened through good management and leadership, but the core values must be there when you hire them or you will lose a lot of time and effort trying to make unqualified and unmotivated people into the stars you want them to be.

As with any pyramid if you do not have a solid base, then you will not have a strong pyramid. If the five attributes listed above do not make up the base of your pyramid as you build an organization, then it will collapse from above. These are the fundamental building blocks of a successful business and they need to be rampant throughout your organization and in the people you hire!

Chapter 6 – Goal Driven

Setting and attaining clear and measurable goals must be a cornerstone of every successful person, and of course, every successful business. Managers at nearly every organization set specific goals each year, especially as they relate to sales and profitability objectives. Additionally, most organizations set individual goals for each employee to let them know what is expected of them during the upcoming year. Of course there is nothing wrong with group goals or those that are set for individual employees, but a truly successful person in any endeavor will probably not simply accept these goals, achieve them, and do nothing more. Truly successful people will typically create their own internal goals and they will probably be much more ambitious than those that have been assigned to them.

The people that do this are the exact type that you need to bring into your organization. Hopefully, as a business owner/manager it is a trait that you also demonstrate all the time.

An important thing to remember is that goals and the plans necessary to achieve them must go hand in hand. The French writer Antoine de Saint-Exupery once said that *"a goal without plan is just a wish"* and he is 100% correct. From trying to run a successful business by setting goals without a plan is like trying to live with air and no water. You can do it, but you won't be around long! Given the importance of being goal driven AND in creating the appropriate plans, this chapter will cover both topics on an individual basis.

How to set goals

George Doran is typically credited with creating the SMART mnemonic on effective goal writing. He identified five very specific concepts that every goal, whether it is business related or personal in nature needs to take into consideration:

1. **They need to be specific (S)** – Improving customer service levels, while admirable is not a very specific goal. Improving customer service levels by 50% is very specific and will certainly have more meaning to your employees. Strong, specific goals will act as a magnet to people within your organization and help give meaning to your efforts.

2. **They need to be measurable (M)** – As an example, if you want to improve your customer service then you must know what your baseline is by measuring where you are today. If you are rated at 4 out of 10 today and you want to improve this by 50% then you will need to raise your rating to 6 out of 10. Anonymous surveys can help determine exactly how you are viewed by your customer base. Once you take certain steps to improve the situation you must be able to measure your customer service levels after you have implemented the changes. Only then will you be able to determine if you have met your goal.

3. **They need to be attainable, but not something that can be reached too easily (A)** - If you only have a customer satisfaction level of 2 out of 10 then it will probably be unrealistic to think that you can improve it to 9 out of 10 in three months. In fact three months is probably not even enough time to wait before you send out a follow up survey. It is important that you make your goals hard enough that you and your employees have to stretch to achieve them, but not so difficult that you will fail.

4. **They must be relevant (R)** - You may desire to have the best business year in the history of the company, but if the country you work in is in the midst of a recession

and a few new competitors have entered your market then setting this type of goal may not be relevant at all.

5. **They must be timed based (T)** – You need to set a specific deadline for each goal to be achieved. It provides a sense of urgency and helps people focus on making sure things get done on a timely basis.

Examples of being goal oriented

One of the best explanations on the importance of personal goal setting comes to us from Michael Jordan in his book entitled, **I Cannot Accept Not Trying - Michael Jordan on the Pursuit of Excellence**. Although he probably did not do this by design you can see many of the SMART principles in his statements below:

> *"I approach everything step by step....I had always set short-term goals. As I look back, each one of the steps or successes led to the next one. When I got cut from the varsity team as a sophomore in high school, I learned something. I knew I never wanted to feel that bad again....So I set a goal of becoming a starter on the varsity. That's what I focused on all summer. When I worked on my game, that's what I thought about. When it happened, I set another goal, a reasonable, manageable goal that I could realistically achieve if I worked hard enough....I guess I approached it with the end in mind. I knew exactly where I wanted to go, and I focused on getting there. As I reached those goals, they built on one another. I gained a little confidence every time I came through."*

> *"... If your goal is to become a doctor and you're getting Cs in biology then the first thing you have to do is get Bs in biology and then As. You have to perfect the first step and then move on to chemistry or physics. Take those small steps. Otherwise you're opening yourself up to all kinds of frustration. Where would your confidence come*

from if the only measure of success was becoming a doctor? If you tried as hard as you could and didn't become a doctor, would that mean your whole life was a failure? Of course not.

All those steps are like pieces of a puzzle. They all come together to form a picture....Not everyone is going to be the greatest....But you can still be considered a success....Step by step. I can't see any other way of accomplishing anything."

This is quite insightful and most of us can learn a lot from his simple comments on goal setting.

Another person who realized the importance of setting goals was Walt Disney. He was an incredible man whose impact upon American culture is perhaps immeasurable. The characters and images he spawned continue to influence lives throughout the world and his brand consistently ranks as one of the most well-known and strongest in modern history.

Even though he was wildly creative in his own right he recognized that he needed a team of gifted people that could help him get what he wanted, especially if they were all focused on the same goal. Often regarded as a task master and at times a difficult boss, he always knew the value of setting goals, and once had this to say about what it takes to succeed:

"Of all the things I've done, the most vital is coordinating those who work with me and aiming their efforts at a certain goal."

Walt Disney had other goals and one of them was to build a huge amusement park in California. His dream began sometime in the late 1930' or 40's but everything was put on hold due to World War II. Financing was another obstacle because he did not have the resources required in order to create a park that would meet his far flung expectations. Even his brother Roy felt that he was over-reaching and initially rallied against the park's development. One thing never wavered and that was Walt's goal of getting his park built. Step by step he rounded up investors and devised creative ways of finalizing his dream. He created a TV show called Disneyland, which the fledgling ABC network aired in an exchange for help in financing his park. He also realized that he could rent out many of the shops on "Main Street" to outside vendors which he also used to help finalize his dream. None of this would have been possible, had it not been for the simple goal Walt had to create a park that parents could bring their children to, and enjoy a long day of merriment.

Finally, on July 18, 1955 the much heralded park opened to the public. It was the first of many that are now operating throughout the world and they are a true testament to the tenacity, vision and unwavering goals set forth by this remarkable human being.

Personal goals

I recently had a discussion with a college graduate who had just turned 23 years old. Her goal is to have a career that will pay her $130,000 per year by the time she is 30. Where she came up with that figure I have no idea. The key thing, however, is that she set this personal goal and she also indicated that she has each step of what she needs to do, and when she needs to do them completely mapped out. This goal was not assigned to her by her supervisor; it came from within. She inherently recognized that she wanted to achieve more than simply doing her job and attaining her business goals on a day to day basis. I didn't have the opportunity to discuss the details of her plan on attaining this goal, but given her drive and intelligence I will be very surprised if she doesn't reach her objective.

Finding and recruiting people that set these types of personal/business goals will pay long term dividends to most businesses. People that set their own goals typically have a lot of motivation and a desire to succeed. As long as their goals coincide with those of the organization they will undoubtedly be key players in helping a business grow.

Goals give you focus, they allow you to measure your progress, they help you to overcome procrastination, and they most certainly provide motivation.

Obviously, finding people like Walt Disney and Michael Jordan is not easy, but you can find people that understand the importance of setting goals and who have experienced success in doing so BEFORE you hire them. There are people out there like the 23 year old college graduate I spoke with and it will be a big help to your business to find these types of people. Not everyone is taught the importance of goal setting at an early age, but it's a skill that can be developed as long as find the right people with the right mentality, if you want to help them fully develop this attribute.

If the people on your staff are a good match to attributes from the base of my pyramid then you will be well served to spend additional time helping them set their own personal goals if they have not done so already. Talk to them about Michael Jordan and show them how the utilization of small achievable goals enabled him to achieve greatness.

Planning

Goal setting and planning go hand-in-hand. You cannot create a meaningful plan without goals and you cannot effectively create a plan unless you know what your goal is.

No one should EVER expect to run a successful business without a comprehensive plan. Even if your goal is to sell water to thirsty people in the desert you will not be able to attain success unless you have created a plan to actually locate the thirsty people and then determine the best way in which to distribute the water!

Setting a goal is the easy part. Creating a plan along with the correct implementation is the hard part!

Every business needs to have a number of different plans created at some point. I won't attempt to go into detail on each of these items, but I want to at least provide a list of the most important ones for virtually any business:

1. **General Business Plan** – Everything you need to have in order to get your business off the ground and obtain any necessary financing.

2. **Marketing Plan** – An over-arching statement about your market, competitors and promotional budget.

3. **SWOT Plans** – This will be modified each year and will include every important aspect of your organization along with specific goals and plans. Unfortunately, many Strategic Planning sessions results in a long list of SWOT items with little time spent on the actual plan to capitalize on the strengths and opportunities and to minimize the impact of weaknesses and threats. Please keep in mind that there are a number of excellent tools available to help with the planning process. In the past, I have utilized one called the *Hoshin Policy Deployment Matrix* that I have found useful; and you can easily find data on this tool by searching the Internet.

4. **Individual sales territory plans** - created by each sales person based upon their specific territory and results from the previous year.

5. **Individual employee plans** – these can and should be created by each person outside of the sales team. Every person in the organization should have goals set for them on an annual basis. Each person should then be asked to return a plan on what they intend to do to meet these objectives. These should be reviewed on a quarterly basis in order to ensure that everything is on track.

Since this chapter is geared toward finding and developing people that are goal driven, I wanted to provide a few comments on planning tools aimed at individuals that you might find valuable during your coaching sessions.

Individual sales territory plans

Sales people need to plan what they will do throughout the year in order to meet their goals on an annual basis. Often sales people quickly assemble a plan because their manager requests one, and too often it's nothing more than a bunch of words on a piece of paper. Sadly, managers frequently contribute to the problem because they request a plan at the beginning of the year and then never use it to review what is happening with each individual sales person. It's imperative that you keep this from happening and to ensure that this type of tool is actually used during individual discussions and coaching sessions throughout the year.

Every sales team is different, but there are certain elements that need to be included in any sales plan and one of the most important is the "close rate" for the individual sales person. This is simply the percentage of new opportunities the person has created that resulted in an order. If you created 50 new opportunities and received 10 orders then you have a 20% "close rate". Over time, this figure will become more and more accurate, but I seriously doubt that many sales people have a true close rate over 35%. If you hear differently, especially if it is significantly higher than 30 to 35%, then my guess is that the sales person is not recording the opportunity in your customer relationship management (CRM) system until they are very far along in the sales process. This is typically what I have seen, if and when a sales person states that they have a close rate of 70 to 80% for all of their opportunities.

You can easily create a template in a spreadsheet I to use for your sales territory plan. Below is an example created by one of my previous sales managers, John Pollard. I have modified it slightly and it should provide you with a few topics that you may want to consider for inclusion:

20XX Territory Business Plan	

Sales Rep:	

Annual Budget	$1,000,000
Close Rate	25%
Annual Required Opportunities	$4,000,000
Sales Cycle in Months	6
Quarterly Budget	$250,000
At Any Given Point	$2,000,000

Current vale of open opportunities	$1,300,000
Difference from figurre "at any given point"	$700,000
My Target Date to achieve "at any given point" is:	
Weighted value of open opportunities	
Last Year Territory Revenue	$900,000
Number of Opportunities Created Last Year	100
$ amount of Opportunities Created Last Year	$3,600,000
Number of Opportunities Won Last Year	25
Average dollar amount of opportunities won	$36,000
Number of Opportunities Lost Last Year	40
Number of Opportunities Still Open Created Last Year	35

YTD Sales Budget	$ 250,000
YTD Actual Sales	$ 200,000
Diffrence to budget YTD	$ (50,000)
# Of Opportunities Created YTD	15
$ Amount of Opportunities Created YTD	0
Average # Of Activities Created YTD	70
Average # of Monthly Customer Visits	15

The information in the sample data above is hopefully self-explanatory. It's up to you as the business owner/manager to determine what aspects are important for your organization. I recommend that you discuss the situation with your sales manager or other trusted advisors to come up with criteria that will be beneficial to your company. Having identified this, here are some additional items that you may also want to consider:

1. If I am currently behind budget on a year to date basis, what specific things will I do between now and the end of our fiscal year in order to fix the situation?
2. Summary of the reasons why I lost orders last year and what can be done this year to fix the situation.
3. Individual Territory Strengths and Territory Weaknesses
4. Last year market strengths
5. This year my focus markets will be...
6. What specific things do you think you can do to become a better sales person? In what areas do you feel that you are strong and where can you use some development? What type of training do you feel that you will need? What will you do to rectify the situation?
7. How many workshops or seminars will you perform in your territory? (This may not be suitable for all sales people)
8. How many hours/days per month are you going to allocate each month to database clean up? This includes updating competitive information, completing a customer profile that will be added to the CRM, and adding/updating email addresses? Remember to reflect this on your calendar.
9. How many hours/days per month are you going to allocate each month to prospecting. This is above and beyond searching web pages for on-line bids and RFQ's.
10. Top 10 accounts in my territory for which I do not have a sales opportunity started. Future dates to contact each one should be included.

Individual plans for people outside of the sales team

Every person in every department should know what their goals are for the upcoming year. These goals need to be in-line with the overall corporate goals and the ones for the specific department in which they work. Once the goals have been agreed upon and established then each individual should be responsible for creating their own plan on attaining these goals.

For example:

IT technician has a goal to reduce technology costs by 15%. The written plan could include how they will obtain quotes from three new computer vendors by the end of the first quarter in order to reduce the amount of money being spent on laptop and desktop computers.

Or

Your accounts receivable clerk has been challenged with reducing your overall receivables by 10%. Part of the plan might be to immediately utilize the new CRM/ERP system to keep track of outstanding accounts so that the system will automatically remind them to follow up BEFORE they become past due.

Every organization and every person will have different goals given the environment in which they work. If you have created your own goals, developed an honest evaluation of your situation, and identified what you know and don't know, then an individual plan should be relatively easy to create.

Remember, you must get your team members to recognize they are responsible for their own success. Help everyone to understand that if they create a well thought out plan and then never follow it they will have no one to blame for their lack of success but themselves.

If you happen to work for an organization that does not require individual sales/business/marketing plans create them anyway. It will help you manage your day to day work in an effective manner and it will also help demonstrate to your supervisor that you are serious about your success. Remember to ask employees to review it with you as it will begin an important dialogue that may not normally occur. Your supervisor may be able to point out some areas that you have missed or make some suggestions on other aspects of your performance that you should focus on. If ever there was a win-win situation this is it. Other than a little bit of work every committed employee should want to create an annual plan.

Your manager may like your concept so much that he will ask your colleagues to prepare the same thing. Be aware that some of the less committed members of your team may not be very happy!

Goal setting and planning worksheet

There are many worksheets that have been created to help people outline their individual goals and plans for the future. If you do not have any tools that you can use to coach your team members, then I hope you will consider the items below. They are a simple example of a personal goal setting and planning tool that many people have found to be effective.

Personal Development Plan

Name: _____ Manager: _____

Position: _____ Date: _____

How long in current role: _____

Career Plan – Personal Vision Statement

Short Term Goals (1-2 Years)	
Area of Interest/Title	Knowledge Needed – Areas for Development

Long Term Goals (3-5 Years)	
Area of Interest/Title	Knowledge Needed – Areas for Development

Personal Development Plan

Strength to Build Upon Identify at least one strength on which to build upon		Focus Area		
What critical behaviors do I need to exhibit for this skill?	Action Steps Remember SMART	Manager's Role or other person if necessary	Target Dates	Examples of how I have adapted my behavior or skills

The fields above read in the following fashion:

Personal Development Plan

Strength to Build Upon
Identify at least one strength on which to build
Action Steps – Remember SMART

Focus Area
Manager's Role or other person if necessary
Target Dates
Example of how I have adapted my behavior or skills

Goal setting and planning are keys to the long term success of every organization AND to the people that work there. Hopefully, as a business owner/manager you already recognize this as an important aspect and that you spend an appropriate amount of time on the process. It is extremely important that you find other people that share this viewpoint and to help them develop their skills in this area. You will be amazed at the results you can achieve if everyone on your team is goal oriented and has a plan for success.

Management Checklist

- ✓ Do I have clearly stated goals and plans not only for my business, but also as an individual?
- ✓ Do I frequently review these goals and plans to ensure that we are on the road to success, or are they simply words on a piece of paper?
- ✓ Does everyone on my team understand the importance of business and personal goal setting and am I doing everything that I can do to help them achieve success?
- ✓ Are my goals flexible and do I have the courage to make the necessary adjustments when appropriate?

Note: Some of the forms and graphs that are contained in this book may be a bit difficult to read since they were converted from color into black and white. For this reason, I have created a website that contains copies of each one for further review. The URL follows:

http://chrissopko.wix.com/pobs

"Failing to plan, is planning to fail" – **John Wooden**

"There are people who put their dreams in a little box and say, Yes, I've got dreams, of course I've got dreams. Then they put the box away and bring it out once in a while to look in it, and yep, they're still there." - **Erma Bombeck**

"If you don't know where you are going you will end up someplace else." – **Yogi Berra**

Chapter 7 - Customer Focused

Happy and satisfied customers are the lifeblood of every organization and without them no business can be successful over the long run. It is imperative then, that your customers are always the main focus of your organization and that they feel happy each and every time they have an interaction with someone from your organization. If you cannot do this then your business will begin to suffer. If you need proof of this, please take note of the following information:

- It costs five times more to attract a new customer than to keep an existing one. (Source: seehosting.com)
- 68% of customers leave because they were upset with the treatment they receive. (Source: Small Business Administration)
- 48% of customer who had a negative experience told 10 or more other potential customers. (Source: Harvard Business Review)
- 64% of customers cited "shared values" as a reason for a strong brand relationship. (Source: Corporate Executive Board)
- It takes 12 positive experiences to make up for one negative experience. (Source: Ruby Newell-Legner, "*Understanding Customers*")
- 59% of Americans will try a new vendor in search of a better customer service experience. (Source: American Express)

Keeping your existing customers happy is unbelievably important, but another key thing to remember is that your customers are not just the people that purchase your product. They're also the people that work within your organization; and if you don't already, then you should begin to think of them as your internal customers. Most businesses that are even mildly successful recognize the importance of having happy and satisfied external customers, but too often fellow staff members (internal customers) are overlooked.

A significant portion of this chapter deals with keeping your external customers happy, but much of the information has application for both groups. The last section entitled "how to improve your customer service" can certainly have a positive impact on your internal customers. A lot more information pertaining to your internal customers, however, is included in the chapter on "Team Building".

Customer service

An old maxim that still has credence today, identifies the three rules to great customer service, which follows:

1. The customer is always right
2. If the customer is not right, then see rule #3
3. Refer back to rule #1

This focus on keeping customers happy likely began within the hospitality industry and most of the successful organizations within that arena continue to focus a considerable amount of their efforts on this old adage that "*the customer is always right*".

Why? Because it works.

If a customer is happy you can expect the following:

- They are more likely to purchase again in the future, or to recommend your product to a colleague.
- It is certainly an easy way in which you can differentiate your organization from your competitors.
- It reduces customer defection to your competitors.
- It increases the total lifetime customer value and thus the profitability of the customer.
- It reduces negative feedback in the marketplace.

- It is ALWAYS cheaper to keep a customer than to find a new one.

A happy and pleased customer within the hospitality industry will come back again and relatively soon. An unhappy customer means that they will not return and they will probably tell at least 10 of their friends about their experience. This type of word of mouth *"advertising"* can make or break a business within the hospitality industry quite quickly.

This type of customer immediacy may be quite different within a business-to-business environment, because sales typically do not take place quite as frequently. Someone selling copiers to a small business may only sell one machine to an organization every 5 to 10 years. The same can be said for people selling equipment to an analytical laboratory, or those selling point-of-sale systems to the hospitality industry. This lack of frequency sometimes causes poorly run organizations to lose focus on the importance of customer service, but it is a critical mistake for ANY and EVERY business, regardless of their customers purchasing patterns.

Great customer service examples

Some organizations are known for their customer service and much can be learned from their experience. The American Express Website listed this example:

> ### Trader Joe's Braves a Winter Storm for an Elderly Customer
>
> *An 89-year old Pennsylvanian was snowed in around the holidays, and his daughter was concerned he wasn't going to have enough food to last the inclement weather. The daughter called multiple stores trying to find someone who would deliver, and finally learned that Trader Joe's doesn't normally deliver, but it would in this special instance. It took the order, and also suggested*

other items that might fit the elderly man's special low-sodium diet.

After the daughter ordered around $50 worth of food to be delivered, the Trader Joe's employee told her that she didn't need to pay for it, and to have a Merry Christmas.

The food was delivered within 30 minutes of the phone call, and the holidays were saved for one elderly man and his family

Another great example, listed on mentalfloss.com

Apple

This story was all over the place after the launch of the iPad 2 a few years ago. Apparently a man bought an iPad online, then returned it to the company almost immediately, affixing a Post-It to the front of the device that simply read, "Wife said no." Returns processors must have gotten a kick out of it, because the story eventually made its way to a couple of Apple VPs, who refunded the customer and returned the iPad with an attached Post-It that said, "Apple said yes."

A final example from the legend in excellent customer service as reported by Christian Conte:

Nordstrom

There was a member of the housekeeping staff at a store in Connecticut who discovered a customer's bags, along with her receipt and a flight itinerary, in the parking lot.

Noticing that the customer had likely left directly from the store to catch her flight at John F. Kennedy International Airport in New York, he looked up her phone number in the company's system and tried to call her several times as he drove to the airport with her bags.

When she didn't answer her phone after he got to the airport, the employee had the airport page her to let her know he had her bags.

These examples underscore what it takes to provide great customer service. This needs to be a focus for every business and continually emphasized with each and every employee. Depending upon your specific business you may not always be able to control the quality or delivery of the product you are selling. What you can control, however, is how you interact with your customers and the level of service that you provide to them.

Things to keep in mind regarding great customer service

1. **Know who the boss is** – In case you are struggling with this it is the customer. EVERYONE in an organization needs to understand that they are in business to service their customer regardless of the industry or what type of organization it is.
2. **Listen to your customers** - Take the time to ask questions of your customers and find out what is important to them. This can be done through individual conversations, phone surveys or on-line questionnaires. Obviously, the best (although least efficient way) is to speak directly to each customer. This allows you to experience the tone of their voice, their body language and get a better idea of how they truly feel. Seek out your customers thoughts, especially after a sale takes place!
3. **Make customers feel appreciated** – Too often customers rarely hear from a sales person or members of an organization once a sale has been made. This only goes to alienate customers and make them feel that they are not appreciated for anything other than the

business they brought to your organization. Take time to follow up with customers and make sure that they are happy with you and your organization. Sponsor customer appreciation events. With all of the wonderful CRM tools that are in existence now a days it is very easy to create an automated reminder to call specific customers just to let them know that you were thinking about them and that you wanted to make sure they were happy.

As president at one of my previous organizations, I sent hand written notes to customer that had recently purchased equipment from our company. I thanked them for their order and the confidence they had placed in our company. I asked them to contact me personally if there was anything I could do and I provided my business card and mobile number. In the years that I did this, I got numerous emails and calls from customers letting me know how much they appreciated the note and stated that they had never gotten anything like this from another vendor.

4. **Recognize when you make a mistake and make it right** - No matter how well any business is run mistakes will be made. People know this and can accept errors if they are acknowledged and if the person/company that made the mistake takes the appropriate action in rectifying the situation. In fact, if you handle these issues well you can actually strengthen your relationship with your customer. If a customer sees that you are genuinely trying to fix their problem and acting in a quick, professional manner, they will recognize that you are part of an organization that believes in its customers. They will certainly keep this in mind the next time they make a purchasing decision.

5. **Treat your employees/colleagues well** – As identified earlier in this chapter, every organization has external AND internal customers. Employees are your internal

customers and need to know that they are appreciated just as much as your external customers. It is well known that happy employees make happy customers, so start your customer service efforts within your own organization. Create an employee recognition program that identifies and honors exemplary performance. Allow the employees to be involved in nominating their colleagues for a job well done. You will be surprised at how much enthusiasm this generates, especially when the recognition is given in front of their team members.

At an employee meeting, I was in the middle of a PowerPoint presentation on the importance of customer service and I passed out blank pieces of paper and pens to everyone in attendance. I then asked everyone on my team to complete the following three statements:

1. I work for…
2. The most important person at our organization is…
3. The person who pays my salary is…

By now you should recognize that the right answer is "the customer". Try this within your own organization. You may be surprised by the answers you receive.

Business impact

A high level of customer satisfaction has a demonstrable, positive, impact upon the stock prices of publicly traded companies, who all too often think that customer service must be sacrificed for the bottom line. This is not the case as evidenced by a study that began in the year 2000.

The CFI Group created a stock portfolio to examine the relationship between customer satisfaction and financial success in the short and long term, using data from the

American Customer Satisfaction Index (ACSI), *and the* **National Customer Satisfaction Index UK (NCSI)**.

According to the study, "the cumulative return of a $100 investment in the ACSI fund from April 2000 to April 2012 was $490, a gain of 390 percent. By comparison, the S&P 500 returned only $93, a 7-percent loss.

In the United Kingdom, the NCSI portfolio earned a return of 59 percent from April 2007 to June 2011, and the FTSE 100 had a negative return of 6 percent." In addition, higher levels of customer satisfaction are tied to high levels of positive cash flows with low volatility, and positive earnings surprises.

I wanted to provide one last bit of information regarding the benefits of a strong customer focus which comes from Joe Nocera at *the New York Times* in 2005. It is a bit lengthy, but the message is extremely important.

My Christmas story — the one I've been telling and retelling these last 10 days — began on Friday, Dec. 21.

It was early in the morning, and I had awoken with the sudden, sinking realization that a present I had bought for one of my sons hadn't yet arrived. It wasn't just any present either; it was a PlayStation 3, a $500 item, and a gift, I happened to know from my sources, that he was hoping for.

Like most things I buy online, the PlayStation had come from Amazon.com. So I went to the site and tracked the package — something, thankfully, that is a snap to do on Amazon. What I saw made my heart sink: the package had not only been shipped, it had been delivered to my apartment building days earlier and signed for by one of my neighbors. I knocked on my neighbor's door, and asked if she still had the PlayStation. No, she said; after signing for it, she had put it downstairs in the hallway.

Now I was nearly distraught. In all likelihood, the reason I hadn't seen the package earlier in the week is because it had been stolen, probably by someone delivering something else to the building. Even if that wasn't the case, the one thing I knew for sure was that it was gone — for which I could hardly blame Amazon.

Nonetheless, I got on the phone with an Amazon customer service representative, and explained what had happened: the PlayStation had been shipped, delivered and signed for. It just didn't wind up in my hands. Would Amazon send me a replacement? In my heart of hearts, I knew I didn't have a leg to stand on. I was pleading for mercy.

The Amazon customer service guy didn't blink. After assuring himself that I had never actually touched or seen the PlayStation, he had a replacement on the way before the day was out. It arrived on Christmas Eve. Amazon didn't even charge me for the shipping. My son was very happy. So, of course, was I.

Amazon was not always viewed in a positive light by Wall Street as Mr. Nocera goes on to illustrate:

… Wall Street began to see Amazon in a decidedly different light. It was just another retailer, the bears said, that happened to sell goods online — and had immense, unanticipated infrastructure and technology costs. Its founder and chief executive, Jeffrey P. Bezos, spent huge sums of money on such "frills" as free shipping, which depressed its operating margins. Indeed, those margins — which got as low as 3 percent — were more akin to Wal-Mart's than that of a big-time tech company.

At one point, in mid-2000, a bond analyst named Ravi Suria made his bones by predicting that the company could run out of cash. The stock dropped into single digits.

So when I looked up Amazon's stock price after my little Christmas miracle, I was amazed to see that it had risen around 140 percent last year. (It closed yesterday at $88.79.) The company grew somewhere around 35 percent in 2007, with revenue likely to come in around $15 billion, and well over $1 billion in free cash flow. Its margins had risen to around 6 percent, and it consistently made money.

When I spoke to analysts and investors, they had all kinds of reasons for Amazon's performance last year. "They finally reached a point where their R&D spending was not expanding as fast as their revenues," said Citigroup's Mark S. Mahaney. He and others also talked about Amazon's success in international markets, its fast-growing (and high margin) merchant market, which allows merchants to sell goods alongside Amazon, and its rapidly expanding Web services business. Mostly, though, the investing community pointed to those healthier margins as the main reason for the stock's run-up. Legg Mason's legendary fund manager, Bill Miller, who has made a small fortune for his investors by betting big on Amazon, told me that "Wall Street is almost fanatically focused on margin expansion and contraction."

But I couldn't help wondering if maybe there wasn't something else at play here, something Wall Street never seems to take very seriously. Maybe, just maybe, taking care of customers is something worth doing when you are trying to create a lasting company. Maybe, in fact, it's the best way to build a real business — even if it comes at the expense of short-term results.

It is almost impossible to read or see an interview with Mr. Bezos in which he doesn't, at some point, begin to wax on about what he likes to call "the customer experience." Just a few months ago, for instance, he appeared on Charlie Rose's talk show to tout Amazon's new e-book device, the Kindle. Toward the end of the program, Mr. Rose asked the chief executive an open-ended question about how he spent his time, and Mr. Bezos responded with a soliloquy about his "obsession" with customers.

"They care about having the lowest prices, having vast selection, so they have choice, and getting the products to customers fast," he said. "And the reason I'm so obsessed with these drivers of the customer experience is that I believe that the success we have had over the past 12 years has been driven exclusively by that customer experience. We are not great advertisers. So we start with customers, figure out what they want, and figure out how to get it to them."

Anybody who has spent any time around Mr. Bezos knows that this is not just some line he throws out for public consumption. It has been the guiding principle behind Amazon since it began. "Jeff has been focused on the customer since Day 1," said Suresh Kotha, a management professor at the University of Washington business school who has written several case studies about Amazon. Mr. Miller noted that Amazon has really had only one stated goal since it began: to be the most customer-centric company in the world.

In this, it has largely succeeded. Millions of people instinctively go to Amazon when they want to buy

117

something online because they have come to trust the company in a way they trust few other online entities. Amazon's technology, its interface, its one-click buying service — they are all incredibly easy to use. Its algorithms offer "suggestions" for further buying that actually appeal to its customers. Its Amazon Prime program — for a $79 annual fee you get two-day free shipping — is enormously popular. Unlike what happens at certain other technology companies, when you have a problem, the customer service telephone number isn't hard to find. It is even willing to correct mistakes that it didn't make, as I discovered over Christmas.

All of this, however, comes at a price. Indeed, as I've written before, customer service isn't cheap. Certainly, a fair amount of the hundreds of millions of dollars Amazon has spent on R&D has gone toward developing, say, the Kindle, but a good deal of it has also gone toward improving the customer experience. Amazon is willing to lose money on some of its most popular items like the latest Harry Potter novel. And even with Amazon Prime, it must surely swallow millions of dollars in shipping costs. Indeed, in a presentation to analysts in late November, the company's chief financial officer, Thomas J. Szkutak, showed one slide that read, "Over $600 Million in Forgone Shipping Revenue." And that was just for one year.

Wall Street, however, has never placed much value in Mr. Bezos' emphasis on customers. What he has viewed as money well spent — building customer loyalty — many investors saw as giving away money that should have gone to the bottom line. "What makes their core business so compelling is that they are focused on everything the customer wants," said Scott W. Devitt, who follows Amazon for Stifel Nicolaus & Company. "When you act in that manner many times Wall Street doesn't appreciate it." ***What Wall Street wanted from Amazon is what it always wants: short-term results. That is precisely what Dell tried to give investors when it scrimped on customer service and what eBay did when it heaped new costs on its most dedicated sellers. Eventually, these short-sighted decisions caught up with both companies.*** *(My emphasis)*

But Mr. Bezos refused to give in. "He was spending his time on long-term value creation," Mr. Miller said. There aren't many chief executives who can so easily ignore the entreaties of the investment community, but Mr. Bezos turned out to be one of them. Of course it helps that he owns over 100 million shares of the stock — and is the company's single largest shareholder.

And it also helps that his dogged pursuit of a better customer experience has turned out to be exactly right. Yes, it's true that its international business has been growing rapidly, but that's not the only reason Amazon is back in high-growth mode. Amazon says it has somewhere on the order of 72 million active customers, who, in the last quarter, were spending an average of $184 a year on the site. That's up from $150 or so the year before. Amazon's return customer business is off the charts. According to Forrester Research, 52 percent of people who shop online say they do their product research on Amazon. That is an astounding number.

There is simply no question that Mr. Bezos's obsession with his customers — and the long term — has paid off, even if he had to take some hits to the stock price along the way. Surely, it was worth it. As for me, the $500 favor the company did for me this Christmas will surely rebound in additional business down the line. Why would I ever shop anywhere else online? Then again, there *may be another reason good customer service makes sense. "Jeff used to say that if you did something good for one customer, they would tell 100 customers," Mr. Kotha said.*

I guess that's what I just did.

In the spring of 2014 Amazon stock was trading at $295 with a 52 week range extending to over $400! It seems that Jeff Bezos is on to something, especially as it relates to customer service!

If you want to build a world-class organization then an emphasis on customer service must be at the very core of how you do things. Your long term success is dependent upon keeping your internal and external customers happy. Hire people that share this attitude and recognize how important the customer is to your long term success. Create training programs and seminars based upon providing great customer service. Teach it, live it, breathe it... It will be a wise and worthwhile investment.

How to improve your customer service

Many ideas exist on the best way to improve your customer service. Below eight things that you should consider implementing if you truly want to increase your level of customer service.

1. **LISTEN to your customers** - Give your customers an easy ways to provide feedback on your company, your product, and your customer service. Today's technology allows for nearly instantaneous feedback from customers. You can add a link to an online survey or feedback form to every email that you send out that will give customers the opportunity to let you know how you are doing. You can also make it easy to provide feedback by phone, email or filling out a form on your website. It is amazing today how many companies do

not allow this type of feedback, or that hide sections on how to reach customer or technical support. When companies do this it sends a clear message to their customers that they really do not care about making them happy.

2. **Review EVERY complaint or comment about your customer service** - Make sure that EVERY comment or complaint is read by the appropriate person within your organization, and ensure that the customer receives an appropriate and timely reply.

3. **Take Action** – Create a team of internal people to review these complaints and comments and make sure that they take action on rectifying the situation. One of the worst things you can do is to let customers register their issues and then take no action to fix things.

4. **Communicate** – Keep customers informed. Acknowledge any complaint or issue you get from a customer and let them know what you are doing to fix the situation. Most customers are realistic and will understand if you are not able to immediately make something perfect. They simply want to know that their complaint has been heard and that someone within your organization is taking steps to fix things.

5. **Communicate again** – Create a program that automatically sends a follow up questionnaire after a certain amount of time to customers that have registered a complaint and ask if they have noticed any improvement. If you happen to hear back from the customer that the situation continues to exist, then you as the owner or business manager MUST immediately step in and figure out where things have fallen apart.

6. **Establish an environment where great service is recognized** - Create an internal program that honors and recognizes people on your team that display great acts of customer service.

7. **Focus, focus, focus** – As a business owner or manager you must make it clear to everyone in your organization

how important customer service is and the emphasis it must play within your company. Have frequent staff meetings where good customer service elements are discussed so that this remains in the forefront of their thinking. Show them the comments you received from customers both good and bad and ask them for ideas on how to make things better. Remember not to single out anyone in front of their colleagues if they received a negative comment from a customer. Obviously you need to address the situation, but speak to the person involved with the customer complaint privately. Public humiliation never contributes to the resolution of any problem.

8. **Lead by example** - As a business manager/owner you need to continually show respect for every person at every level in your company. These are your internal customers and you need to help them feel comfortable, secure and recognized as valuable contributors to the long term success of your organization. It is also important for you to NEVER publicly give an indication that an external customer is being too demanding or difficult. This sends a very poor message that it is okay to think of customers in this fashion, which only goes to hurt the level of customer service that they will receive.

Management Checklist

- ✓ How much time do I spend reinforcing the importance of customer service within my organization?
- ✓ Have I created any internal programs to recognize outstanding customer service?
- ✓ Do I clearly show my teammates how much I value them as contributors to the success of my organization?
- ✓ Do I know how my organization is actually viewed by our customers in terms of satisfaction levels?
- ✓ What programs, if any, are in place to improve customer service?

"It is not the employer who pays the wages. Employers only handle the money. It is the customer who pays the wages." – **Henry Ford**

"Customer service is not a department, it's everyone's job" - **Anonymous**

"We see our customers as invited guests to a party, and we are the hosts. It's our job every day to make every important aspect of the customer experience a little bit better" - **Jeff Bezos, CEO Amazon.com**

Chapter 8 – Team Builder

From the previous chapter I hope that the importance of having a strong focus on satisfying your customers is clear. I touched upon the fact that every organization has internal and external customers and this chapter will focus on the topic of building a strong team and how it relates to your internal customers.

Quite simply, I define teamwork as the ability and willingness to give and receive help. Helping others and being willing to let others help you is a key to the success of any organization. If you have people on your staff that cannot understand this, or do not want to be good team players, then you seriously need to consider whether or not they are worth keeping. Who wants to deal with self-centered people that are only focused on their own well-being?

Poor team members

Unfortunately, over the years I have heard sales managers in some organizations that justify selfishness and a lack of willingness to help others simply because the person in question drives a lot of sales. Somehow the end result seemingly justifies the means. However, I would caution that this is ultimately not a wise decision. Accepting this type of behavior sets the wrong tone for any organization that wants to develop a strong sense of team. If this type of behavior is allowed to continue everyone will see that you are turning a blind eye to the situation simply because the person has met with some sort of sales success. It sends a message to the team that the person in question does not have to play by the same rules and that they are being judged by a different set of standards. From what I have seen throughout my career, this does nothing but kill enthusiasm and the desire to work hard for the rest of the employees.

Most people will be glad to focus on being good teammates if they know that their help and efforts will be reciprocated and appreciated. Just think about how much damage is being done by managers who accept people in an organization who have a "me-first", selfish attitude.

My time in business also tells me that self-centered people are difficult to manage in other areas as well. Sales people with this mentality often feel that since they have been successful in generating sales that they do not have to do the administrative work expected by everyone in an organization. These types of people will typically tell you that they want to be left alone so that they can sell. Sadly, the real reason why they don't want to do administrative work, or help anyone else is because it will not immediately put any money in their pocket. It would be terrible if other people in an organization decided to adopt this same attitude. Can you imagine a customer service person that simply decides not to put in any extra effort to get a "rush" quote out the door for an anxious sales person? Or the field service engineer that shuts her phone off at 5:00pm because that is the hours of operation for the business? If everyone in an organization adopted this type of selfish attitude, business would soon begin to suffer.

Everyone in an organization needs to feel like they are on the same team and that they are all pulling in the same direction. Those who do not want to take part are actually hurting your organization no matter what their individual sales or performance results may be. Take these people aside and discuss the situation with them as soon as possible. Ask them why the act the way they do, and give them a chance to explain their thoughts and actions. Perhaps they do not actually realize how they come across and the impact it is having upon the organization. If this is the case, then you may have a chance at changing their behavior. On the other hand, if they do realize how they are acting and they simply don't care then you have a much bigger problem on your hands.

No matter how successful these people may be, I recommend that you do not allow them to continue to act in this way. It is imperative that you let them know that their actions do not fit well with your concept of running a successful business. Using The Pyramid of Business Success as a visual tool is an easy way to broach this discussion, but they must understand that you are serious, and that their behavior cannot continue. You need to give them an opportunity to change, but keep a close eye on them and how they interact with other team members. If you continue to see them behave poorly then you will have no choice but to remove them from your organization. If you don't they will become an infection to your business; and as we all know untreated infections can kill.

Removing people from an organization should never be taken lightly. No matter what the person did, you'll be creating a significant impact on their life and the lives of their family. Making the decision to do this should never be easy; and if it ever gets that way then you have an additional problem in that you may be losing key aspects of your humanity. I always want to give a person the chance to change. You may find that some of these people do not even realize that they are not performing up to expectations and if this is the case, then you must take responsibility as a manager that the situation exists, and take the appropriate steps to fix the situation. On the other hand, if you have been clear in setting your expectations and the person in question still refuses to comply, then in effect they are saying that they no longer want to work for your organization and are making an overt decision to resign.

Your actions

Business owners and managers need to demonstrate teamwork on a daily basis for a number of reasons. When you display great teamwork it illustrates how important it is to your business and it lets your colleagues know that you care about them as individuals. It is imperative for everyone in a supervisory position to pitch in once in a while at virtually every role in a business. At one of my previous leadership roles I worked in the warehouse for a few days in order to let the other team members know that they were not forgotten and that I valued what they did. Frankly, they could not believe what they were seeing…"the president of the company working in the warehouse"…"what's up with that?" It clearly demonstrated to my team that I was not above doing any type of job within the organization and it certainly helped develop a strong relationship with the other members of the warehouse staff. A very important side benefit occurred in that I quickly became aware that we had some inefficiencies in the department that may have gone unnoticed for a time had I not gone through this effort.

Cross training employees is another way in which to help develop teamwork within an organization. Each person that goes through a cross training process will begin to have a better understanding of the true nature of the other person's job. My experience tells me that many people in an organization often do not realize exactly what other team members do. Cross training helps to fill in the gaps and it can give a new appreciation of the complexity inherent in many roles that frequently go unnoticed.

Business expert, Peter Drucker describes teamwork and cross training in his book **Management,** using an example of a doubles team in tennis in which the players each have a primary position, but not a fixed position. The advantage of building such a team is that one employee can cover part of the tennis court for the other. This easily applies to the business world as well, in that you might cross-train two employees to cover each other's positions and perform as a doubles team in tennis. Hopefully, over time they will each be able to compensate for each other's strengths and weaknesses and ultimately help the other one become better overall. Cross-training employees also gives you flexibility in covering lunch breaks, vacations and other business needs, so it is a very important thing for any business.

Examples of teamwork and team building

Above and beyond simply cross training people to cover for each other, organizations can build specific teams to capitalize on the power of multiple minds to solve vexing business issues. Greenbiz.com cited an article written by Mindy Lubber that illustrates this with an example from Levi Strauss:

> ...they discovered exactly how powerful teamwork could be when they challenged their employees to come up with a way to reduce the amount of water needed to produce their jeans.
>
> Jeans production is highly water-intensive, from the cotton in the denim to the finishing touches that make them fashionable and comfy. Most jeans are washed in industrial washing machines three to 10 times during the finishing process -- and that water adds up.
>
> So the company looked inward to find a solution, tapping an employee group that knows its culture and processes intimately: the design team. "Sometimes the way to achieve a more sustainable design is to rethink a traditional process and find a way to do it better," said Levi's Brand Concepts Director Carl Chiara.
>
> Their breakthrough idea? Stonewash their jeans with just the stones, no water.
>
> "The laundry thought we were crazy," added Chiara, but the team really wanted to "challenge conventions."
>
> That they did, reducing the amount of water used to finish jeans by an average of 28 percent -- and up to 96 percent (just 1.5 liters!) for some styles. That adds up to about 16 million liters of water saved for the 1.5 million pairs of jeans that came out in Levi's spring 2011

collection. The reduced water use also cut its energy bills.

Knocking down walls between companies and the communities where they operate is another must. In addition to avoiding disruptive project delays, it can help build more-loyal workforces and stronger reputations.

Lydia Dishman, a regular contributor to *Fast Company* wrote the following about the giant retail store Target and how they make people feel like they are an important part of their organization:

...mentorship is baked into Target's playbook, to develop leaders that really invest in their own teams. There are customized one-on-one programs that begin at the point of hire that have been perfected to a science. "Everyone is a mentor and mentee. It is one of the fun and exciting parts of [any] job" says Gregg Steinhafel, CEO of Target.

There are also company-wide initiatives to gather feedback and improve things at a granular level. For the latter, all 365,000 team members are encouraged to complete a survey about what's working and what's not. "We get well over 300,000 responses," Steinhafel asserts.

Some 15,000 of those come with written suggestions on everything from strategy to tools. Each are personally read by the head of HR and culled for larger ideas to be presented to the executive team. Then says Steinhafel, "It's our responsibility to act and continue to support the teams."

Healthy conflict

You don't need your entire organization to sit around a campfire singing Kumbaya. On the contrary, some level of conflict and disagreement can be healthy for an organization, especially if it is handled correctly. You certainly don't want people yelling, screaming and swearing at each other, but you must expect that people with passion for a topic will often disagree and sometimes it may cause some internal strife, at least in the short run. The important thing is to make sure that everyone maintains a high level of respect, and that at the end of whatever conflict has taken place that everyone is back on the same page and once again pulling in the same direction.

A nice example of this comes to us from an interview given by Steve Jobs, the former CEO of Apple that has been posted on at least 50 different websites:

> *"When I was a young kid there was a widowed man who lived up the street. He was in his eighties. He's a little scary looking. And I got to know him a little bit. I think he may have paid me to mow his lawn.*
>
> *One day he said to me, "Come on into my garage I want to show you something." And he pulled out this dusty old rock tumbler. It was a motor and a coffee can and a little band between them. And he said, "come on with me." We went out into the back and we got some rocks. Some regular old ugly rocks. And we put them in the can with a little bit of liquid and little bit of grit powder and we closed the can up and he turned this motor on and he said, "come back tomorrow."*
>
> *And this can was making a racket as the stones went around.*
>
> *I came back the next day and we opened the can. And we took out these amazingly beautiful polished rocks. The same common stones that had gone in through rubbing against each other like this (clapping his hands), creating a little bit of friction, creating a little bit of noise,*

had come out these beautiful polished rocks.

That's always been in my mind, my metaphor for a team working really hard on something they're passionate about. It's that through the team, through that group of incredibly talented people bumping up against each other, having arguments, having fights sometimes, making some noise, and working together they polish each other and they polish the ideas, and what comes out are these beautiful stones."

This story really resonated with me because conflict within business teams is all too often viewed as a negative thing. Many people seemingly adopt an attitude that basically states "don't confront me and I won't confront you". But this means that we are placing internal group harmony over long term results. As Steve Jobs alluded to, great ideas are often created in the tumbler of life, where as he put it "incredibly talented people bump up against each other."

The development of teams

Another important thing to keep in mind about team building was illustrated by Bruce Tuckman when he developed his "Team Stages Model" in 1965. His model quickly became widely known as the basis for effective team building, and I feel that it still has value today. During his studies, Tuckman began to discover that there were two features common in small groups, "the interpersonal or group structure" and the "task activity". From this he quickly realized that the groups or teams evolved in four common stages for which he coined the famous terms:

1. **Forming** – The initial stages of team development in which the team has not yet gelled together.
2. **Storming** – People begin to see themselves as part of a team, but they still challenge each other greatly about how and why things need to be done

3. **Norming** – This is where the team really starts to come together and establishes rules, clarifies responsibilities and establishes deadlines.
4. **Performing** – This is the final stage in which people focus on the tasks as well as the continued development of the team itself.

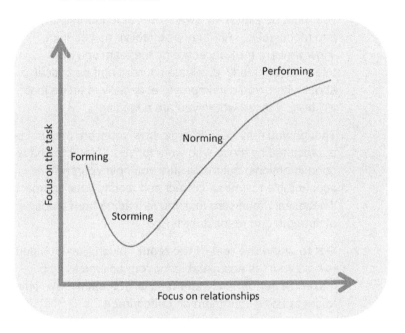

The real value of Tuckman's model is that it gets one to recognize how teams evolve especially when they are assembled to work on a project. There will most certainly be difficulties during the initial stages as Jobs recognized many years later. In fact, team members may seem to be disorganized and at odds with one another, but over time the team will coalesce and perform wonderful things if given the right guidance and leadership. Please keep this in mind as you create teams within your organization and manage them through the process of helping you build your successful business.

How to increase your team building

Glenn Llopis contributed an article to *Forbes Magazine* on how good leaders can help develop stronger teams. I have provided a slightly modified summary of his six steps below:

1. **Be aware of how you work** - As the leader of the team, you must be extremely aware of your leadership style and techniques. Are they as effective as you think? How well are they accepted by the team you are attempting to lead? Evaluate yourself and be critical about where you can improve, especially in areas that will benefit those whom you are a leading.

    Though you may be in-charge, how you work may not be appreciated by those who work for you. You may have good intentions, but make sure you hold yourself accountable to course-correct and modify your approach if necessary to assure that you're leading from a position of strength and respectability.

2. **Get to know the rest of the team** - Much like you need to hold yourself accountable for your actions to help maximize performance and results, you must make time to get to know your team and encourage camaraderie. The importance of caring, understanding the needs of your team, embracing differences and helping your colleagues understand their significance must be discussed. In this case, gathering intelligence means learning what defines the strengths and capabilities of your team. These are the real assets that each member brings to the table, those they leave behind, and those yet to be developed.

    All great leaders know exactly what buttons to push and when to push them. They are experts at activating the talent that surrounds them. They are equally as effective at matching unique areas of subject matter expertise and/or competencies to solve problems and seek new solutions.

Fully knowing your team means that you have invested the time to understand how they are wired to think, and what is required to motivate them to excel beyond what is expected from them.

Think of your team as puzzle pieces that can be placed together in a variety of ways.

3. **Clearly define roles and responsibilities** - When you successfully complete step two, you can then more effectively and clearly define the roles and responsibilities of those on your team. Now, don't assume this is an easy step; in fact, you'll often find that people's ideal roles lay outside their job descriptions.

   Each of your team member's responsibilities must be interconnected and dependent upon one another. This is not unlike team sports, where some players are known as "system players" – meaning that, although they may not be the most talented person on the team, they know how to work best within the system. This is why you must have a keen eye for talent that can evaluate people not only on their ability to play a particular role – but even more so on whether they fit the workplace culture (the system) and will be a team player.

   For example, I once inherited an employee who wasn't very good at his specific job. Instead of firing him, I took the time to get to know him and utilized his natural talents as a strategic facilitator who could keep all of the moving parts within the department in proper alignment and in lock-step communication. This person helped our team operate more efficiently and saved the company money by avoiding the bad decisions they previously made because of miscommunications. He was eventually promoted into a special projects manager role.

A team should operate as a mosaic whose unique strengths and differences convert into a powerful united force.

4. **Be proactive with feedback** - Feedback is the key to assuring any team is staying on track, but more importantly that it is improving each day. Feedback should be proactive and constant. Many leaders are prone to wait until a problem occurs before they give feedback.

    Feedback is simply the art of great communication. It should be something that is part of a manager's natural dialogue. Feedback can be both formal and informal. If it becomes too structured and stiff, however, it becomes difficult for the feedback to be authentic and impactful.

    Every team is different, with its own unique nuances and dynamics. Treat them as such. No cookie-cutter approach is allowed. Allow proactive feedback to serve as your team's greatest enabler for continuous improvement.

    Take the time to remind someone of how and what they can be doing better. Learn from them. Don't complicate the process of constructive feedback. Feedback is two-way communication.

5. **Acknowledge and reward** - With proactive feedback comes acknowledgement and reward. People love recognition, but are most appreciative of respect. Take the time to give your teammates the proper accolades they have earned and deserve. I have seen too many leaders take performance for granted because they don't believe that one should be rewarded for "doing their job."

At a time when people want to feel as if they are making a difference, be a thoughtful leader and reassure your team that you are paying attention to their efforts. Being genuine in your recognition and respect goes a long way towards building loyalty and trust. It organically ignites extra effort!

When people are acknowledged, their work brings them greater satisfaction and becomes more purposeful.

6. **Always celebrate success** - At a time when uncertainty is being dealt with each day, you must take the time to celebrate success. This goes beyond acknowledgment – this is about taking a step-back and reflecting on what you have accomplished and what you have learned throughout the journey.

   In today's fast-paced, rapidly changing world of work, people are not taking enough time to understand why they were successful and how their success reverberated and positively impacted those around them. I have seen leaders fall into the trap of self-aggrandizement – because of what their teams accomplished – rather than celebrating the success stories that in many cases required tremendous effort, sacrifice and perseverance.

   Celebration is a short-lived activity. Don't ignore it. Take the time to live in the moment and remember what allowed you to cross the finish line.

Management Checklist

✓ Do I continually reinforce the importance of building strong teams and in acting as a good team member?

- ✓ As a business owner or manager do I demonstrate the elements of being a good team member as a role model?
- ✓ Do I allow people within my organization to avoid being good team members because they may bring value in other areas?
- ✓ Do I provide feedback and reinforcement for solid teamwork on a continual basis?
- ✓ Do I fully recognize that my internal customers are just as important as my external customers and do I demonstrate that to them through decent wages and a good working environment?

"Talent wins games, but teamwork and intelligence wins championships." **- Michael Jordan**

"Teamwork is so important that it is virtually impossible for you to reach the heights of your capabilities or make the money that you want without becoming very good at it." **- Brian Tracy**

"Alone we can do so little; together we can do so much" **- Helen Keller**

Chapter 9 – Excellent Communicator

Success in business is greatly impacted by the ability to effectively communicate. Without effective communication you can't convey your goals, sell your products, or coach your internal teams. Thousands, if not millions of books have been written on communication and I certainly will not attempt to cover this entire topic. I want to help you understand the dramatic importance of *"effective"* communication, however, and to recognize that what happens in business on a daily basis is often something entirely different.

Poor communication

A perfect example of less than perfect communication was posted on the CNN website:

> *(CNN) -- NASA lost a $125 million Mars orbiter because a Lockheed Martin engineering team used English units of measurement while the agency's team used the more conventional metric system for a key spacecraft operation, according to a review finding released Thursday.*
>
> *The units mismatch prevented navigation information from transferring between the Mars Climate Orbiter spacecraft team in at Lockheed Martin in Denver and the flight team at NASA's Jet Propulsion Laboratory in Pasadena, California.*
>
> *Lockheed Martin helped build, develop and operate the spacecraft for NASA. Its engineers provided navigation commands for Climate Orbiter's thrusters in English units although NASA has been using the metric system predominantly since at least 1990.*

No one is pointing fingers at Lockheed Martin, said Tom Gavin, the JPL administrator to whom all project managers report.

"This is an end-to-end process problem," he said. "A single error like this should not have caused the loss of Climate Orbiter. Something went wrong in our system processes in checks and balances that we have that should have caught this and fixed it."

That's right...poor communication cost NASA a $125 million dollar Mars orbiter!

Another example

Social Media is a huge part of the marketing budget for many businesses throughout the world, but poor execution can have huge negative impacts as demonstrated by the following example:

A tweet was sent out from Kenneth Cole's Twitter account in 2011 in an attempt to promote their new spring fashion collection. It was immediately deemed to be offensive, insensitive, and it outright offended millions of people. Meant as a bit of humor, the corporate tweet turned out to be nothing more than a poor play on the political turmoil happening at the time in Egypt:

Home Profile Find People Settings Help Si

Millions are in uproar in #Cairo. Rumor is they heard our new spring collection is now available online at http://bit.ly/KCairo -KC

about 5 hours ago via Twitter for BlackBerry®

KennethCole
Kenneth Cole

According to sources, the tweet actually came from the Chairman through the Kenneth Cole corporate Twitter account. After the immediate, negative feedback the company took down the tweet down and quickly apologized to anyone that they had offended. Many lessons can be learned from this mistaken communication, one of which is to give serious thought to any corporate communication BEFORE it leaves your organization.

My own mistakes

Early on in my management career I made a huge blunder in communicating with one of my department heads. She was a long term, very loyal employee who had been promoted up the ranks into a significant management role. Unfortunately, she had not been given much theoretical management training and the results from her team often suffered from her lack of leadership. She would actually take it upon herself to complete the work that was supposed to be done by her team members instead of holding each of them responsible for getting things completed. On numerous occasions she indicated that she would rather not be a manager if she had to force people to complete their assignments. This person simply could not muster the internal fortitude necessary to get her team to take responsibility for their work, and felt more comfortable in simply completing the jobs herself.

I tried on numerous occasions to get her to change her management style but it was clear that I would never fix this situation. I certainly didn't want to lose this person, but it was also obvious that I needed to make a management change. I brought her into my office and told her that I needed to make a change. I said it was clear that she was overwhelmed, that her group was struggling, and that I had decided to bring in another manager for the department. I told her that she would still be in the group, but that the new person would be responsible for managing the people in the department, assigning tasks, and making sure that things got done on a timely basis. Much to my surprise she seemed to be relieved and very supportive of my decision. From my standpoint, it must have been obvious to her that things were not getting done, which is why I thought she openly welcomed the opportunity to have someone else take on these responsibilities.

As it turns out I had communicated my intentions in a very poor fashion. What she heard was that I was bringing in a new person to "help" manage the group and she did not realize that she would no longer be the manager. She assumed that she would still be in charge of the department and the new person would handle those administrative and managerial responsibilities that she was unable or unwilling to complete. It was not clear to her that she would simply be an employee within the department and that the new person would become the new manager of the entire group, including her.

What I should have done was to state that she was no longer going to be the manager of the department in a clear and concise fashion instead of simply identifying that I was bringing in another manager. I should also have provided her with a follow up document about our discussion that included the details of how the department would be managed in the future. It might sound strange, but my poor verbal communication and lack of follow up in writing left the door open in her mind that there would be two managers of the same department.

Listening

During my research for this chapter I often found "listening" listed as the number one item required for effective communication. The website skillsyouneed.com identified the following comments on how to improve your listening skills which will most certainly be worthwhile to review.

1. ***Stop Talking*** *- Don't talk, listen. When somebody else is talking listen to what they are saying, do not interrupt, talk over them or finish their sentences for them. Stop, just listen. When the other person has finished talking you may then takes steps to clarify and ensure that you have received their message accurately.*

2. ***Prepare Yourself to Listen*** *- Relax. Focus on the speaker. Put other things out of your mind. The human mind is easily distracted by other thoughts – what's for lunch, what time do I need to leave to catch my train, is it going to rain – try to put other thoughts out of your mind and concentrate on the messages that are being communicated.*

3. ***Put the Speaker at Ease*** *- Help the speaker to feel free to speak. Remember their needs and concerns. Nod or use other gestures or words to encourage them to continue. Maintain eye contact but don't stare – show you are listening and understanding what is being said.*

4. ***Remove Distractions*** *- Focus on what is being said: don't doodle, shuffle papers, look out the window, pick your fingernails or similar. Avoid unnecessary interruptions. These behaviors disrupt the listening process and send messages to the speaker that you are bored or distracted.*

5. ***Empathize*** *- Try to understand the other person's point of view. Look at issues from their perspective. Let go of preconceived ideas. By having an open mind we can more fully empathize with the speaker. If the speaker says something that you disagree with then wait and*

construct an argument to counter what is said, but keep an open mind to the views and opinions of others.

6. **Be Patient -** *A pause, even a long pause, does not necessarily mean that the speaker has finished. Be patient and let the speaker continue in their own time, sometimes it takes time to formulate what to say and how to say it. Never interrupt or finish a sentence for someone.*

7. **Avoid Personal Prejudice -** *Try to be impartial. Don't become irritated and don't let the person's habits or mannerisms distract you from what they are really saying. Everybody has a different way of speaking - some people for example, are more nervous or shy than others, some have regional accents or make excessive arm movements, some people like to pace while talking - others like to sit still. Focus on what is being said and try to ignore styles of delivery.*

8. **Listen to the Tone** - *Volume and tone both add to what someone is saying. A good speaker will use both volume and tone to their advantage to keep an audience attentive; everybody will use pitch, tone and volume of voice in certain situations – let these help you to understand the emphasis of what is being said.*

9. **Listen for Ideas – Not Just Words -** *You need to get the whole picture, not just isolated bits and pieces. Maybe one of the most difficult aspects of listening is the ability to link together pieces of information to reveal the ideas of others. With proper concentration, letting go of distractions, and focus, this becomes easier.*

10. **Wait and Watch for Non-Verbal Communication -** *Gestures, facial expressions, and eye-movements can all be important. We don't just listen with our ears but also with our eyes – watch and pick up the additional information being transmitted via non-verbal communication.*

Email

One of the biggest sources of miscommunication in the workplace comes from the use of email. Although it's one of the quickest and most immediate tools for communication, it's also one of the most misconstrued methods. Many people don't realize the importance that non-verbal clues place in how a message is interpreted. Dr. John Lund, author and business consultant on communication strategy, recently stated that that we interpret messages based upon the following three things:

- 55% is based on their facial expressions and their body language.
- 37% is based on the tone of their voice.
- 8% is based on the words they say.

Think about this. In normal communication we interpret 92% of the message based upon facial expressions and tone of voice and only 8% on the words that were uttered. This means that the significant bulk of communication takes place outside of the words that have actually been spoken!

With more than 520 million emails sent each day, this can result in so much misinterpretation of the actual message of an email because the recipients have no way to see the other person's body language and hear the tone of their voice.

Think about how many times you send an email and the person responds in a fashion that clearly indicates that they misconstrued what you were trying to convey. I hate to admit it, but despite my best efforts it still happens to me on occasion. For this reason alone, it's imperative that managers communicate important information in as direct a fashion as possible. Granted face-to- face communication is often impossible due to the size and geographic breadth of many organizations, but a wise manager will use other tools to help avoid as much miscommunication as possible; especially regarding important topics.

A hierarchy of the best ways to communicate follows:

1. Face -to-face communication
2. Utilizing tools such as Skype or Facetime for one on one interaction.
3. Individual phone calls
4. Group conference calls/webinars
5. Email/Electronic Communication
6. Regular mail or registered mail depending on the circumstances.

But most times, the items on this list are flip-flopped in the business world. How many times do emails get sent out on important matters that are misconstrued and misunderstood by the recipients?

Even if you have a face-to-face meeting or an individual phone call you should always provide those that you are communicating with a detailed document that outlines what you have just discussed. This gives the recipient something to refer to in the future in case they forget what was said in person.

Common communication mistakes

Please consider the items below and how they can lead to communication issues:

- **No specific deadline** - You send an email to a colleague asking them to deliver an important report to you by Thursday. You get a clear reply that she will have no problem getting you the information by Thursday. On the surface, this might seem like an example of good communication, but the employee might think she has until 5 p.m. to deliver the report when you actually need it first thing on Thursday morning. This can create a huge issue especially if this is an important report needed for someone higher up in the organization or for a customer. The important thing is to remember to always give a detailed deadline whenever you communicate a need. If it is extremely important, then you should also schedule a pre-deadline discussion to ensure that everything is on track.

- **Missing important details** - Not providing specific deadlines is just one example of how things can go awry from a communication standpoint.   Please keep in mind that any important communication should include a review of the standard "who, what, when, where, how and why" to avoid miscommunication and to ensure that your message covers all of the important bases.

- **No response** – Remember that just because you do not get a response does not mean that you are being ignored. This is especially true for email being sent outside of your organization. Email messages often end up in a spam file, fail to get sent correctly, or get buried and lost under the hundred other messages your recipient receives.   If you have an important message to send by email always ask for a response, or make a follow-up confirmation call.

- **Casual communication** - It's not uncommon to briefly stop by a group of employees as you pass them in the hallway and simply say to one of them *"Oh..by the way, can you please ..."*

While you may think you are giving your employee a direct order or specific task, that employee might be headed out the door or into another meeting. Unplanned distractions happen all of the time so there is no guarantee that the person has truly understood your message. A better tactic might be to simply ask them to stop by your office when they are done with their conversation in the hallway. This will ensure that you and the person receiving your message will have the time and focus to ensure that everyone is on the same page.

No one sets out to miscommunicate with others. Unfortunately, the negative impacts upon a business include decreased productivity, low morale, and general mistakes. Taking a few extra moments to speak directly with a team member will help keep these things from happening. If email is required, then make sure to be specific and cover the "who, what, when, where and why" before you send the message.

Effective communication helps all of us understand each other better and it enables everyone on a team to help resolve their inherent differences. It also aids in building trust, respect, and it fosters an environment where creative ideas, problem solving, and teamwork can flourish.

As often as we do it every day, much of what we communicate to others gets misunderstood, causing conflict and frustration in all our relationships, whether they are personal or professional. Learning and practicing effective communication skills will pay huge dividends throughout every organization regardless of the size or structure. It just takes a little bit of time and effort.

An open door policy

Having an open door policy is one thing that many organizations talk about with their employees. However, this type of situation in which anyone in the organization can walk in and discuss issues or problems with their supervisor on up to the president of the company does not often take place.

In theory it is a wonderful idea, but it takes a lot of time and open minded people on your management team to make it effective. The key is to create an open environment in which everyone feels comfortable in expressing their opinion, even if is different from the prevailing view. The worst thing that can happen is for someone to go to their supervisor and to be told that their idea was poor or that they were trying to discuss some taboo subject within the organization.

If this happens people will immediately let others in the company know how they were treated and it will create an environment in which no one wants to openly discuss anything. This is one reason why I like to have an employee meeting at least once per month so that I can let everyone in the organization know how the business is doing. It also allows people to ask any questions that they may have in mind. Sometimes it may be difficult for people to ask tough questions, especially at first so you may want to have an anonymous comment box available. This will give your entire team the opportunity to ask questions that they may not feel comfortable asking in person. If as a manger or owner you handle the situation correctly and calmly answer the question; people will start to recognize that your "open door policy" and your desire for honest communication are sincere.

I can't stress enough how important creating this type of positive environment is in building a successful organization. As a group, your people see everything that is going on in your organization, both good and bad. It is imperative that you make each of them feel welcome to share their thoughts and suggestions with you on how to make your business better and more profitable. You will be surprised at the great ideas that your team can come up with, especially if they are operating in environment of open and frank communications.

10 steps to become a better communicator

1. **Be receptive** – Every discussion has some sort of goal, but if you are too interested in what you need to accomplish you may not be hearing important details coming from the person you are talking to. It is important not to be closed minded and to actually HEAR what the other person is trying to convey. This is what is meant by listening, yet it is more than simply listening to words. It is creating an environment in which you truly understand the intent and meaning of what is being said.

2. **Read between the lines** - A lot can be learned from the way in which a person is communicating with you or in the non-verbal cues you give off during a conversation. The way you move your hands, the intonation of your voice, and your lack of eye contact, all mean something when having a dialogue with another person. These non-verbal cues can be easy to misinterpret, so it is imperative for you to remember this and to keep it in consideration, especially during important conversations.

3. **Maintain a positive attitude** – Having a discussion with someone while angry leads to many instances of miscommunication. It is important to remain as positive as possible when having a discussion, because negative emotions can make you misinterpret the intention of the other and not listen to them as earnestly as you should.

4. **Show the other person respect** – No matter how difficult a conversation may be, the other person also has their opinion and feelings. A key to avoiding miscommunication is to keep this in mind so that you can maintain a high level of respect for the other person regardless of their opinion. Losing respect for the person you are communicating with is the quickest way to let the conversation devolve into a shouting match.

5. **Never interrupt** - We all want to make our point, but unless you need to interrupt to clarify something important, then it is much better to remain silent and let the other person finish. Constantly interrupting the other person indicates that you do not value what they have to say and that you feel that your thoughts are more important. Interrupting the other person is also a sure fire way for increased miscommunication and in making the other person angry.

6. **Clarify** – If you are unsure of what the other person means, then ask for clarification. This is probably one of the biggest inhibitors of effective communication because one person hears something that may be entirely different from what the other person meant. One solid suggestion in these situations is to try and repeat back to the person what you thought they just said and meant. You may be surprised at how often you have misconstrued the situation.

7. **Mirroring** - Many studies have been done on the importance of mirroring and how it seemingly improves face-to-face communications. If the person you are talking to moves forward, then you should move forward. If they put their hands on the table then you should put your hands on the table and so on. For some reason, this type of mirroring makes the other person feel more comfortable about the conversation. Obviously, you do not want to overdo it, but it may help you facilitate a better conversation with someone.

8. **Planning** – If you know you need to have an important discussion with someone then plan out the types of questions you may want to ask in advance. Preparation will make you more confident and it will also ensure that you have covered all of the points necessary. Try and ask a lot of open ended questions that will solicit more than one word, yes and no answers. The more dialogue

that you can have the better the communication will be, especially if it is focused and on point.

9. **Be sincere** – Sincerity is a key to successful communication. If people know that your heart is in the right place and that you really mean what you are saying then they will be more open to your message. If they think you are insincere and as some people say, "*blowing smoke up their butts*" then you will quickly lose your ability to have effective communications.

10. **Be confident** – No one wants to follow a person that is wishy-washy and can't make up their mind. When you have something important to say, then say it. You need to be respectful and plan out what you want to communicate, but confidence in presenting the message is half the battle.

So much of effective communication comes back to how believable you are as a person. If you have always acted with honesty and integrity then you will certainly be more believable to the people that know and respect you. As a result, the people that you are talking to will be more open to your ideas and to perhaps make the changes you may be suggesting. If people doubt your sincerity or do not trust you then nothing that you say or do will have much effect until you can get your credibility back.

Management Checklist

✓ Do I actually listen to people with differing points of view or do I feel so strongly in my beliefs that I ignore their thoughts?

✓ Do I let my teammates know that I want to have open and honest communications with them at all times?

✓ When faced with a tough question or dialogue do I lose my temper and make people feel uncomfortable?

✓ If I honestly evaluate my current situation, how many times do I hear differing points of view? Is that because all of my ideas are brilliant or because people do not feel comfortable discussing them with me?

✓ Do I try and communicate important messages face to face, or do I simply send out an email that can be easily misconstrued?

"The single biggest problem in communication is the illusion that it has taken place." - **George Bernard Shaw**

"Precision of communication is important, more important than ever, in our era of hair trigger balances, when a false or misunderstood word may create as much disaster as a sudden thoughtless act." – **James Thurber**

"You can have brilliant ideas, but if you can't get them across, your ideas won't get you anywhere." – **Lee Iacocca**

Chapter 10 - Competitive

Every business owner or manager needs a certain level of internal competitiveness if they want to have a successful, long term business. Even if you currently have the greatest product on the market you will need to be competitive enough to continue to develop something new, or the people you are selling against will ultimately surpass you, and your business will soon decline. This is just one aspect of being competitive, but it extends into many other areas of a business which is why this chapter is important.

Being competitive means you are aware of how everyone else in your marketplace may currently be doing something, and figuring out a better way to accomplish the same thing. Some people refer to this as "building a better mouse trap". It also means keeping your eyes on what the competition is doing and using whatever advances they may be making as a *"burr in your saddle"* in order to keep pushing yourself and your organization to new heights. Without a competitive spirit this will typically not be done too well. Being a competitor means that you will have the mental toughness to push through difficult situations to remain successful. This closely relates to resilience. But being competitive is more than just being able to recover from setbacks. It's about having an internal drive to be the best, and to create an environment that includes a group of people with a will to win against the competition.

Matt Blair, a competitive cyclist had this to say on the matter:

> *"Being competitive is a requirement to survive and be successful. In order to succeed, we must embrace our competitive nature, challenge ourselves, and overcome the obstacles that keep us from our dreams".*

How true!

Internal competition

Some recent studies have been published that indicate that internal competition within a business is actually a bad thing. After reviewing the data, it is clear to me that it was not the competitive environment that caused the problems but how the competition was introduced and managed with the employees. Internal competition can't be cut throat. It must not create an environment of "us versus them" in which various groups or departments are actually hoping that others on the team fail. This will not be healthy for any business and it'll create an adversarial and negative environment.

A good manager can and should be able to create a healthy level of competition within an organization that will assist in pushing everyone on the team to new heights and not cause divisiveness. Sales people should most certainly be compared to their colleagues about their results, but teamwork should never be forgotten. Warehouse workers can be divided into internal teams to compete on who can ship the most orders with the lowest number of errors. Similar "competitions" can be created in which people are rewarded for receiving high customer service marks. These are just some of the small things you can do to create some internal competition and help your people and business develop.

You can be successful in creating a program of internal competition, but you must remember to present the situation in the right fashion. Make it clear to your team that you are creating the competitive environment to *increase* **teamwork and performance** and *NOT* to pit one person against another. You must let them know that you will not accept this type of behavior and then reinforce it on a daily basis. If your rationale, explanation, and management of the competitive environment are clear, then I believe that it can be incredibly healthy for an organization. Competition, teamwork and integrity can go hand-in-hand and it is your job as a business owner to create and foster this type of environment within your organization.

Creating a competitive environment is not strictly about winning. It is about performing to the best of our abilities, creating advantages over what is currently offered in the market and having the desire, will and tenacity to implement the changes necessary to successfully compete. If you can create a healthy competitive environment at work it will most certainly pay dividends. Maggie Chingombe published an article that outlined her thoughts on the matter:

1. **Goal and deadlines** - Goals are usually met where there is competition. This is because your best achievers are motivated by achieving set goals, objectives or deadlines.
2. **Production** - Production is increased where there is competition. As the employees compete, they also increase production in their quest to outdo one another. Where employees are competing in teams, teamwork is enhanced greatly. They learn to communicate effectively and assist one another to achieve the team's set goals.
3. **Improved work quality** - Competition also leads better quality work. This is because an employee cannot be recognized as the best if their work is shoddy.
4. **Self-improvement** - As employees compete, they also find ways to improve their own performance. They can seek training, get more organized and eliminate things that waste their time.
5. **Work oriented staff or teams** - As employees compete with one another, they become more work oriented. Work becomes more important to them.
6. **Higher profits** - As productivity increases due to competition the company also performs better and achieves higher profits.

General benefits of competition

Much can be learned from the world of athletics, especially as it pertains to the benefits of competition and the impact it can have upon your business. Pat Rigsby, one of the founders of Fitness Consulting Group identified a list of things that he has learned through the competitive nature of athletics. They all certainly have application in the business world and I have added a notation at the end of each bullet point to identify their relation to various chapters in this book.

- *The Ability To Handle Adversity – you can't go very far as an athlete without having to overcome adversity and the most successful athletes are usually the ones who deal with adversity the most effectively.* (Resilience)
- *Work Ethic – I remember my freshman year of high school going to baseball practice at 3:15 after school and being done at 8. It was kind of a rude awakening for a 14 year old, but I quickly learned that to be successful you couldn't do just enough to get by. I don't know anyone who has ever become a real success just punching the clock and working 9-5.* (Hard Work)
- *The Intangibles Matter As Much As The Tangibles – Many of the most talented athletes I've ever played with or coached were huge underachievers when it came to performance. They didn't have the passion, drive or willingness to work hard. They couldn't handle adversity. To this day – I'll hire intangibles 10 times out of 10 over a great resume.* (Hard work, Resilience, and Competitiveness)
- *To Keep Score – The beauty of sports is that you keep score. There is a tangible way to measure performance. I tracked everything when I coached because I was looking for an edge. We track our numbers for the same reasons now – if you don't keep score you can't measure how you're performing and know where to*

focus your efforts on improvement. (Goal Driven and Competitiveness)

- ***Sacrifice & A Team Attitude*** *– If you compete in a team sport and want to succeed at a high level you quickly learn to work within the framework of a group, sacrifice some of your individual goals for the good of the team and understand that if you want to be a champion you need to get past selfishness and shortsightedness.* (Team Builder)
- ***You Can't Hide*** *– As a baseball player, if you step in the batter's box it's a moment of truth. You either put in the hours in practice or you didn't. As a coach, when your team takes the field – you either recruited and did the job preparing your team – or you didn't. Too many people make excuses. Sports teach you that excuses don't get you very far.* (Personal Accountability)
- ***Hustle Can Make Up For A Lot*** *– As a player I got to play at a higher level than my talent probably would have taken me because I worked hard. As a coach we developed a nationally ranked program with some of the worst resources in the country. If you're willing to outwork the competition you can overcome a lot of shortcomings – whether it is talent, resources or anything else.* (Hard Work)

Every item on his list is related to various chapters throughout this book, which is just one reason why I believe that having a competitive nature will pay dividends for any business owner. Being competitive does not mean that you have to be a jerk. John Wooden is a prime example of how you can be extremely competitive and driven, yet maintain a healthy outlook and a strong sense of team building. As a business owner/manager, you can certainly have a drive and desire to be the best in your markets without lying, stealing and without degrading the competition.

Successful competitive examples

There have been many famous instances where athletic and business competitors leveraged their desire and competitive spirit to drive each other and their customers to new heights. The following stories should provide inspiration on the benefits of competition and further reinforce the idea that being competitive doesn't have to mean giving way to negative feelings and hatred:

Bill Gates and Steve Jobs – By Adam Lashinsky

Bill Gates and Steve jobs were as different as night and day, yet they had much in common. This probably explains their rivalry.

The fruits of their enmity? The creation of the personal computer.

First, the differences: Gates was an upper-middle-class kid who went to Harvard. Jobs grew up in a family of modest means and didn't attend many classes at Reed College. Deeply technical, Gates wrote the code for Microsoft's early products himself. A born marketer with enough technical chops to be persuasive, Jobs relied on collaborator Steve Wozniak to create the first Apple computer. Gates was the poster child for geeks everywhere. Jobs, meanwhile, was suave from the start. Gates understood scale and leverage; Jobs grasped style and message. (The more charismatic figure, Jobs, will have been played on film by both Noah Wiley and Ashton Kutcher.)

Gates and Jobs became the opposing poles of the frantically growing computing revolution. Above all else, though, these rivals understood business. Neither had formal training in the black arts of balance sheets and income statements. Indeed, neither had graduated from college. Yet both were preternaturally shrewd about making a buck -- and how to win against the competition. Gates dominated the first two decades of their rivalry, overseeing Windows' rise as the world's default operating system.

Eventually Jobs welcomed a $150 million investment from Gates in 1997 when Apple was looking death in the face. In fact, attendees of the Macworld conference where the deal was announced booed Gates' appearance by video. But during the last 15 years of his life, Jobs flipped the switch on Gates, dominating beyond-the-PC segments like music players, smartphones, and tablets -- all areas of heavy, and mostly fruitless, investment by Microsoft.

The two were known to trade not-so-subtle barbs. Jobs diagnosed Microsoft's essential problem as a lack of taste. Meanwhile, Gates summed up one of Jobs' greatest achievements, the iPad, by saying simply, "it's okay." Born seven months apart (Jobs was older), they were friendly in the years before Jobs died. Having fought each other for so long, they knew better than anyone what the other had accomplished.

Apple has been the most valued company in the world for a number of years and Microsoft continues to dominate the market for operating systems and business software. Few would argue that the competition between these storied companies did not have a positive effect upon each company in their own way. Where would Apple would be if Bill Gates had not had the fortitude to loan his competitor $150 million in their time of need?

Michigan vs Ohio State (College Football) – Bentley Historical Library – The University of Michigan

Of all the coaching match-ups in the long Michigan-Ohio State rivalry, none has been more intense and at times bitter than that between Woody Hayes and "Bo"

Schembechler. For ten years the two dominated the "Big 2 and Little 8," splitting ten conference titles between and finishing second eight times. Hayes supposedly could not bring himself to speak the name of "that school up north" and Schembechler, who played for Hayes at Miami of Ohio and was an Ohio State assistant coach, savored nothing more than putting it to his old mentor. After a decade of memorable on-field stratagems, sideline antics, and locker room psychological ploys, the two coaches came out almost dead-even, Schembechler holding a slim 5-4-1 advantage.

Even more significant is how the two legendary coaches actually felt about each other despite their fierce rivalry, which is often referred to as the greatest in all of sports.

Woody on Bo:
"If 'Bo' is not a winner, I never saw one and I should know. He beat me the last three games we played. We've fought and quarreled for years but we're great friends." [Quoted in The Lantern February 10, 1986.]

Bo on Woody:
"There was plenty to criticize about Woody Hayes. His methods were tough, his temper was, at times, unforgivable. And, unless you knew him or played for him, it is hard to explain why you liked being around the guy. But you didn't just like it, you loved it. He was simply fascinating." [From Bo by "Bo" Schembechler and Mitch Albom.]

Despite their competitiveness and desire to win there was a tremendous amount of respect between these two giants of college football. Schembechler once stated that Hayes was the first person to arrive at his hospital room after he had a heart attack. Would anyone do this if they did not truly care about the other person? The two were unbelievably competitive, yet they were also great friends. Why can't this type of environment be created in the business world? The answer: It can!

Larry Bird and Magic Johnson - National Basketball Association (NBA) – National Public Radio 2009

In the 1980s, the Boston Celtics and the Los Angeles Lakers dominated professional basketball, winning a combined eight titles during a decade that was known as the "golden era" of the NBA.

The modern-day NBA would not be what it is without the era's superstars — Hall of Famers Larry Bird of the Celtics and the Lakers' Earvin "Magic" Johnson — and the rivalry that elevated the entire league.

In a new book, When the Game Was Ours, co-written by Jackie MacMullan, Bird and Johnson detail their love and hate for one another over the years. Johnson says that after competing against each other in the 1979 NCAA championship game, they joined NBA teams that already hated each other.

"We're so competitive anyway that there was a dislike there," Johnson tells NPR's Michele Norris. "I even hated him more because I knew he could beat me."

The rivalry between the two teams started in the 1950s — and Bird says he and Johnson "rekindled the fire."

"We did it in a way where we caught the imagination of everyone in America," he says. "People wanted to see us play against one another. ... If you like competition you want to play against the best, and that's what we wanted to do."

A Defining Lunch

Then in 1985, Converse asked Johnson and Bird to tape a shoe commercial in French Lick, Ind., Bird's hometown. Johnson says he agreed to it, but he was nervous because he had never had a conversation with Bird.

"I'm nervous! I'm nervous!" he says. "It's like I'm going crazy, like, 'What's going to happen?' "

During the shoot, the two didn't talk. But then a curious thing happened: They bonded over lunch at Bird's house.

"His mom gave me the biggest hug and hello, and right then she had me," Johnson says. "Then Larry and I sat down for lunch, and I tell you, we figured out we're so much alike. We're both from the Midwest, we grew up poor, our families [are] everything to us, basketball is everything to us. So that changed my whole outlook on Larry Bird."

Johnson's teammates and coach couldn't believe the two had lunch.

"Believe me, everybody was shocked," he says.

Bird said he was nervous about getting too close to his rival.

"I always thought you had to keep the edge," he says. "You don't want to get too close to a person because you will get a little soft. Once me and Magic left that commercial shoot in Indiana, it was back to business, believe me. We both had a burning desire to win *championships. And once we got with our teams, all of that was forgotten until we retired."*

The Diagnosis — And Phone Call

Then, on Nov. 7, 1991, Johnson called Bird and told him he had been diagnosed with HIV. Bird was on the short list of his basketball colleagues to tell before he got in front of the camera and shocked the nation.

"We'd been connected to each other since college," Johnson says. "We were always thinking about each other — what we were doing and how we were doing. I knew that he would want to know and also know from me. And I'm glad I was able to talk to Larry and let him know that I'm gonna be OK, and I knew he was going to be supporting me."

Bird says he'll never forget the moment he got the call.

"It was probably one of the worst feelings you could ever imagine," he says. "It was very difficult. We played against each other for a long time. At that time, HIV was known to be a death sentence. But for some reason, when he told me he was going to be fine, I believed him because everything he's ever said had really come to be true, as far as winning and winning championships. So I felt a little bit better. But still — I was a gamer, I loved game day; I couldn't wait to get down to the gym. But when I got that call that's the one time I can honestly say I didn't feel like playing."

Johnson said he needed Bird in that moment — and he knows he can count on him, even if they see each other only once a year.

"Both Larry and I are very strong, strong-willed, strong-minded," he says. "Sometimes that armor is weakened. As strong as I appeared to be, I still needed a friend to just say, 'Hey man, I'm here, I'm supporting you. Just do what you got to do to be here for a long time.' You don't have to talk every day and we don't. But we know that if I need something, he's gonna be there. If Larry needs something, I'm gonna be there. And he knows that. And then when we do get together — when I see Larry and I get that pound, and I get that hello — I'm good. It takes me through my next year or two, until I see him again."

Remarkable! Two of the most heavily decorated basketball players in the second half of the 20th century became very close friends despite the fact that competed against each other at the highest level for nearly 20 years. They also stated that the mere presence of the other person and how hard they worked pushed them to increase their efforts at becoming better basketball players. This story once again illustrates that even the most hardened competitors can rise above their differences to attain long lasting friendships. This is just one more example of the importance of a competitive nature and how it can be utilized in a positive fashion.

Competitive about everything in your business

The application of your competitive spirit should apply to all activities including creating your SWOT analysis, marketing plan, new product development, or how to incentivize your team to name just a few. This type of constant evaluation and change is not always an easy task and unless you have a burning desire to make it happen brought on by a competitive spirit it may be hard to remain motivated throughout everything it entails.

You have to bring this competitive spirit to your organization and try to surround yourself with others who also share this attribute. By doing so, you will be creating an environment geared toward success!

Steps to create healthy competition at work

As a manager it is your responsibility to ensure that any competition in your organization is healthy and not destructive. It can be a fine line, but it most certainly can be done with a little effort. Here are a seven items that you should consider before implementing any form of competition with your workforce:

1. **Explain the overall goal** – It's important for everyone to understand why any and every competition has been set up. The goal is to make each individual better at what they are doing and to ultimately make the organization stronger and more profitable. This can also mean developing a stronger sense of teamwork within the organization. This concept needs to be continually stressed BEFORE, DURING, and AFTER any competition.

2. **It has to be healthy competition** – It's imperative for everyone to know that the competition is "with" their team members not "against" their team members. You do not want anyone to root for the failure of another person in the organization so that they can win. This does nothing but create animosity and needless, unproductive tension.

3. **Seek feedback** – Ask your team members what type of internal competition can be devised that will strengthen the organization. Remember to stress that the goal is to make everyone better and not to root for the failure of the other team or individual team members. Let them play a key role in setting the objectives to ensure that it will be productive and most importantly "fun".

4. **Consider making your competition based upon improvements in individual performance** – This can give everyone some impetus to improve their performance.

167

5. **Allow for additional goals and prizes** – You may want to reward people in the competition that showed the most team spirit or teamwork in helping others in the organization. This is a great way to keep the competition from becoming cut throat.

6. **Make winning valuable** – Make the prizes well known and readily identifiable. Rewards based upon arbitrary factors will kill morale. Everyone must have a feeling that they can be a winner or at least part of a winning team. Don't forget to make the prizes valuable to the people taking part in the competition. A $5 gift card to Starbuck may be of little interest and value to your team members.

7. **Not every competition has to be business related** – Valuable competitions can be created that can pay big dividends to an organization even though they may not be directly related to business issues. Fund raising contests can create a lot of comradery and make people feel good about themselves and the organization. You may want to also create a competition on quitting smoking or on a weight loss program. All of these types of competitions that do not directly affect the business can be very valuable in creating a strong sense of teamwork, which in the long run is great for everyone.

Management Checklist

- ✓ Am I constantly using my competitive spirit to make my business run more efficiently?
- ✓ Have I created a healthy environment for internal competitions to increase productivity and teamwork?
- ✓ Do I get my team involved in setting up competitions, or do I try to make the decisions on my own?
- ✓ Do I discuss the benefits of competition with my teammates to ensure that they understand the benefits it can bring to our organization?

✓ Do I ensure that any internal competition program does not create negative feelings within the organization and that they always result in positive situations?

"A competitor will find a way to win. Competitors take bad breaks and use them to drive themselves just that much harder." - **Nancy Lopez**

"Competition in business is a blessing, for without it, we wouldn't be motivated to improve." - **Nabil N. Jamal**

"The best competition I have is against myself, to become better." – **John Wooden**

Chapter 11 – Sound Judgment

We all know that today's business world is an ever changing and increasingly complex environment. Given the circumstances, it's incredibly important for a business owner/manager to continually display a high level of sound judgment to help guide an organization through what can often be difficult times. Despite the best plans and written policies, managers are forced to make daily decisions that can have a huge impact upon a business, and there will undoubtedly be times when mistakes are made. The key as a good manager/owner is to minimize the number of poor decisions by utilizing sound judgment at all times; and to add others to your team that also display this characteristic.

I once reported to a manager who used to say, "If everything can be covered by a policy manual then you don't need managers" and he is 100% correct. Policy manuals are guides on how things should operate. They certainly cannot cover every situation that will arise. Everyone should be aware of what the policies are, but sometimes it's necessary to step outside of the policy, which is why it's necessary to find people that demonstrate sound judgment over and over again.

Types of decisions

There are three categories of business decisions that an owner/manager is typically faced with:

1. **Day–to-day decisions**– These are relatively quick decisions often pertaining to employees, customer situations, and vendors. These are items such as whether or not to extend a warranty to a customer or if you should let someone leave early to take care of a sick child, etc. These are also the types of decisions that

really test how closely your decisions match to the items at the base of the Pyramid of Success. They will stick with your employees and customers and give them a true representation of your core values. Although they are individually small in nature they have a cumulative effect that can set the tone for your entire organization. No matter how much you stress the importance of being honest and acting with integrity if you do not display it when making daily decisions it will ring hollow and you will lose credibility. The same can be said with displaying enthusiasm, resilience and holding yourself accountable. If you do not display these characteristics time and time again as these decisions unfold then your people will not either.

2. **Longer term decisions** - Longer term decisions will steadily guide the company to success and are typically based upon facts, market research and sound judgment. Sometimes these decisions are made as part of a strategic planning process. Other times they are based upon known facts and at times assumptions based upon historical knowledge of your markets and industries. These can be things like making a decision to hire a new sales person and where they should be placed geographically. It might also mean making a decision to terminate an employee, and/or how to price a new product being introduced to the market. Anyone who has ever been in a leadership position will tell you that these types of decisions are not always clear cut and obvious. Sometimes there will be multiple options and they will all be beset with risks and uncertainty. At some point, you will simply have to make a decision and rely on your experience and your history of sound judgment.

3. **Big picture/broad changes** – These are decisions that affect the very core and future of an organization. They may be significant enough to cause a complete re-direction of an organization. Facts and market research are a big part of these types of decisions but often times

it is the drive and vision of a key leader that makes it possible to move the organization in a new direction.

In order to illustrate these types of decisions, I have included a summary by the editors of *Fortune Magazine* of a book entitled **"The Greatest Business Decisions of All Time"**. The details below will provide some clarification and inspiration:

Great Decision #1 - 1914: Henry Ford decides to double his workers' wages

Lesson Learned: With their pay doubled, Ford's autoworkers could now afford the very products they were producing. This triggered a consumer revolution that helped create the wealthiest nation on earth.

Henry Ford had a problem. He was becoming too successful. The growing popularity of the Model T was causing him to rethink his ideas about mass production. He had introduced the moving assembly line at his Highland Park, Mich., plant in 1913, and it had worked far better than he could have imagined. The year before the assembly line was installed; he had doubled production of the Model T by doubling the size of his workforce. The following year he nearly doubled production again, but this time he did it with the same number of workers. The assembly line had made the plant so efficient that the Highland Park payroll actually fell.

The trouble was, employee turnover was accelerating at an alarming rate. The dispiriting, mind-numbing work on the line was causing workers to quit en masse. The men (and it was all men back then) reacted to their narrowly defined, repetitive, and physically demanding jobs by leaving them.

Acting on the advice of his devoted lieutenant, James Couzens, Ford decided to take radical action. On Jan. 5, 1914, Ford and Couzens summoned newspaper reporters to the plant to publicize changes in employment policies at Highland Park that they hoped would improve employee retention. First, the company would reduce the workday from nine hours to eight. Second, it was moving to three shifts a day instead of two, opening up lots of new jobs. But the big news came in the third announcement: Subject to certain conditions, Ford would more than double the basic rate of pay to $5 a day. The 11-year-old company was willing to spend an additional $10 million annually to improve productivity and the lives of its workers.

The news spread quickly beyond southeast Michigan. "A magnificent act of generosity," declared the New York Evening Post. But the Five-Dollar Day turned out to be an excellent investment. Within a year, annual labor turnover fell from 370% to 16%; productivity was up 40% to 70%. Between 1910 and 1919, Henry Ford reduced the Model T's price from around $800 to $350, solidified his position as the world's greatest automaker, and made himself a billionaire.

And by raising wages he expanded the overall market for the Model T. As Ford said to reporters that January: "We believe in making 20,000 men prosperous and contented rather than follow the plan of making a few slave drivers in our establishment millionaires."

Great Decision #2 - 1991: How Intel got consumers to love its chips

Lesson learned: *By deciding to brand its product "Intel Inside," the chipmaker proved that an anonymous* *ingredient of a consumer product might achieve its own identity and provide a competitive edge.*

A PC is made of various components: the power unit, keyboard, mouse, hard disk, and -- the brains of the operation -- the microprocessor. Way back when, users of a Compaq no more knew who had supplied those ingredients than a Chevy owner knew who had made the radiator under the hood.

Intel changed all that in 1991.

Until then, the high-tech marketing landscape had pretty much consisted of Apple's rainbow logo and IBM's Little Tramp. But if a small blue Chiquita sticker could turn a banana into a marketing icon, then why not an Intel Inside logo on a computer?

The genesis for "Intel Inside" came from inside the cubicle of CEO Andy Grove. His young technical assistant, Dennis Carter -- who had two engineering degrees and a Harvard MBA -- understood that the company faced challenges in the maturing microprocessor market. The surprising cause: the very success of the microprocessor. Because of Moore's law -- which holds that the number of transistors on a chip roughly double every 18 to 24 months -- Intel and other chipmakers were able to quickly make obsolete each generation of chip. So Intel's 16-bit microprocessor -- called the 286 -- was replaced within three years by the 386, a 32-bit one.

Trouble was, nobody was buying it; everybody was still wedded to the 286 chip, although the 386 was a much better product. Carter wondered whether the problem was that end users weren't aware of the product differences. Grove had his doubts, but in early 1989 he

*agreed to a $500,000 test, telling Carter, "You believe it -
- you go do it." Intel took out billboard ads in Denver with
a big, bold "286" inside a circle and a large red "X"
spray-painted over the 286. After a couple of weeks,
another sign went up next to it: a "386" inside a circle.
The message was clear, and those buying PCs got it:
Sales of computers with Intel's 386 microprocessor shot
up. It was a major moment: Carter had shifted power in
the chip industry from the PC makers to a key supplier.*

*Ultimately Carter became head of marketing, his reward
for demonstrating that an anonymous ingredient of a
larger consumer product might achieve its own identity.*

Great Decision #3 - 1952: Boeing bets big on the 707

Lesson learned: *When CEO Bill Allen decided to
launch the 707, he had no orders in hand. He simply
believed customers would buy. It takes courage to wager
a company's future on a vision.*

*Here's a shocker to even the casual student of aviation
history under the age of, say, 75. At the dawn of the Jet
Age, Boeing, one of today's dominant makers of
commercial aircraft, was a nonentity in the business of
building planes for airlines. That's right. In the years
following World War II, when U.S. industry was retooling
for civilian production, Boeing was primarily a maker of
military aircraft. Its famous B-52 bomber and a
companion tanker had proved that the Seattle company
had the right stuff when it came to jet aircraft technology.
But for the airlines, jets weren't commercially viable:
Converting to jet technology would require a massive
investment that could pockmark their bottom line.*

*The safe choice for Boeing would have been to stick to
its defense-industry knitting. That, however, wasn't the*

plan of Boeing's postwar president, William McPherson Allen, who made a prototypical great decision, a "bet-the-company" move on civil aviation in the form of a single product. He was convinced that consumers would cotton to the speed, convenience, and comfort of jet travel and that the real growth would be in the civilian sector of the booming global economy. Allen was so sure of his conviction that he was willing to risk Boeing's financial future on it.

In 1952 he persuaded the Boeing board of directors to invest $16 million in what would become the Boeing 707, the first U.S. transatlantic commercial jetliner and the plane that would alter the course of Boeing's history. The 707 grew to become as much a cultural icon as a transportation vehicle. The swimwear company Jantzen called its swimsuit line the 707. Every U.S. President from Dwight D. Eisenhower to George H.W. Bush flew on an Air Force One that was a modified version of a 707.

All told, Boeing invested $185 million in the 707. According to a 1957 article in Fortune, that was $36 million more than Boeing's net worth the previous year. It was just one plane, but it remade a company, an industry, and the very culture of its time.

These are just three examples of business leaders that had the vision and courage to make decisions that were dramatically different from the norm, but there are many more. Keep in mind these leaders did not simply go through a strategic planning process and use the facts and figures available to make an informed and hugely influential decision. Rather, they stepped outside of the standard thought process of the day and obviously took some very large risks based upon their judgment and their ability to make sound decisions. As we now know, these decisions turned out to be overwhelmingly successful and are now revered in the annals of business history.

The Flipside

When faced with making a tough decision many business owners or managers rely on outside experts to help them through the decision making process. There is nothing wrong with gathering knowledgeable people around you to help with this process, but it's important to remember that even the so-called "experts" can be wrong when evaluating any given situation. I have attached a list of **10 Misguided Quotes** that will add a bit of humor to this chapter and also illustrate how even the brightest minds can have huge lapses in judgment and misinterpret situations that seem quite obvious to us in hindsight.

1. *"If we put out a screen machine, there will be a use for maybe about ten of them in the whole United States. With that many screen machines, you could show the pictures to everyone in the country — and then it would be done. Let's not kill the goose that lays the golden egg."* - **Thomas Edison on movie projectors**

2. *"I think there is a world market for maybe five computers."* - **Thomas Watson, Chairman of IBM 1943**

3. *"The concept is interesting and well-formed, but in order to earn better than a 'C,' the idea must be feasible."* – **Yale University Professor in response to Fred Smith's paper outlining his idea for an overnight delivery service. Fred Smith went on to create FedEx.**

4. *"Who the hell wants to hear actors talk?"* – **HM Warner, Warner Brothers 1927**

5. *"We don't like their sound, and guitar music is on the way out."* – **Decca Records, rejecting The Beatles 1962**

6. *Heavier-than-air flying machines are impossible."* – **Lord Kelvin – President of the Royal Society 1895**

7. *"Professor Goddard does not know the relation between action and reaction and the need to have something better than a vacuum against which to react. He seems to lack the basic knowledge ladled out daily in high schools."* – **The New York Times in response to Robert Goddard and his revolutionary work on rockets 1921**

8. *"The wireless music box has no imaginable commercial value. Who would pay for a message sent to nobody in particular?"* – **Associates of David Sarnoff's in response to his request as the President of RCA to invest in the radio in the 1920's**

9. *"Airplanes are interesting toys but of no military value."* - **Marechal Ferdinand Foch, Professor of Strategy, Ecole Superieure de Guerre**

10. *Computers in the future may weigh no more than 1.5 tons.* – **Popular Mechanics 1949**

The list above, as humorous as it might be, simply illustrates that the best informed and educated people of their day can evaluate a situation and still not be able to make the right decision. This doesn't mean that they were stupid people. Thomas Edison and Thomas Watson are still considered to be titans of their fields and professors at Yale are most certainly still held in high regard. It simply means that the right decision and a clear way forward are not always obvious. Decisions will need to be made in every business regardless if every factor affecting the outcome is known or not. Sometimes these decisions will turn out to be correct, but other times the results will not be as expected. Clearly, the people on the list above made a lot more good decisions than bad ones, but they were absolutely not immune to the inevitable miscalculation and misevaluation that plagues us all.

Below is an excerpt from **Ethics and Integrity: Pinpoint Management Skill Development Training Series** written by Timothy Bednarz that highlights the elements of sound judgment:

> *Developing good judgment is based upon the manager's ability to look at all sides of a problem or issue and to weigh all of the options before a final determination is made. Typically good judgments are:*
>
> 1. ***Fact-Based*** *- Facts form the basis of all sound judgments. While perhaps self-evident, it is all too easy to base judgments upon opinions, assumptions and personal biases. Before a judgment can be made, managers must take the time to firmly establish the truth of the matter and filter out any opinions, assumptions and biases. When at all possible, facts should be fully documented.*
> 2. ***Objective*** *- Sound judgment is based upon an objective evaluation of the facts. Managers must be careful to ensure their emotions, assumptions, expectations, opinions and personal biases do not affect their objectivity. Where possible, managers should step outside of the immediate situation to view the facts from the other person's perspective and gain objective insights into potential solutions.*
> 3. ***Fair and Balanced*** *- Sound judgment requires that all sides and viewpoints be carefully weighed and considered by managers. One pitfall in sound decision making lies in only considering one side of the issue and thereby limiting objectivity with*

opinions, assumptions or personal biases. When this occurs, the decision is intentionally slanted toward one side of the issue without fully considering other viewpoints and insights. When managers are focusing on making ethical judgments, they must consider all sides of the issue and make sure the input they are considering is balanced. When balanced facts and viewpoints are objectively evaluated, the manager is able to arrive at a fair judgment.

4. **Made When Managers Are Emotionally Stable** - *Managers must refrain from making determinations and judgments in an emotionally unsettled state of mind. Decisions made when a manager is angry or hostile will be rash and subjective. Before effective and sound judgments can be made, managers must assure that their emotions are in check.*

5. **Addressing the Needs of All Parties** - *Sound judgments and decisions encompass the needs of all individuals involved with and affected by them. The final judgment should be in the best interests of all parties. Even when tough decisions are to be made, the best interests of all involved must be considered. For instance, if a manager must let an employee go due to poor performance, that decision – when based on facts – may be in his or her best interest. The individual may need a wake-up call or just may not have the necessary skills to be successful in their job, in which case it is best they pursue another profession.*

6. **Carefully Considering All Options** - *Sound judgments demand that managers consider all possible options. When a problem or issue is first considered, only one viable option may be apparent; however, effective managers will explore and consider all possible options before a decision is to be made. Once managers have collected all the*

facts, viewpoints, insights and options, they need to take the time to thoroughly consider all aspects of the problem or issue before a final judgment is made.

7. **Fully Assessing Risks** - *Effective managers fully assess all the risks associated with their decisions and judgments. They are not risk-averse, but instead weigh all facts and make their decisions based upon the judgment yielding the lowest risk and biggest payoff.*

As a business owner or manager it is your responsibility for the final decisions made on behalf of your organization. This responsibility carries a lot of weight because your decisions can affect the livelihoods of many people. Given the gravitas of the situation, serious decisions should never be taken lightly. Therefore, surround yourself with the right people who have a history of sound judgment, go through a solid evaluation process and make your decision. It will take courage, determination and perhaps resilience if things do not go as planned, but it is a necessity for the long term success of any organization.

Management Checklist

- ✓ Have I chosen my management team carefully to ensure that they have the ability to make sound decisions?
- ✓ Do I follow a good decision making process that will increase the likelihood that the decisions I will make will turn out as planned?
- ✓ Do I clearly convey to my teammates how and why certain decisions are being made?
- ✓ Do I have the courage to make tough decisions even if it may go against "popular" consensus?
- ✓ Do I work with my team members to help them develop their decision making skills?

"Whenever you see a successful business, someone once made a courageous decision." – **Peter Drucker**

"On an important decision one rarely has 100% of the information needed for a good decision no matter how much one spends or how long one waits. And, if one waits too long, he has a different problem and has to start all over. This is the terrible dilemma of the hesitant decision maker." – **Robert K. Greenleaf**

"In any moment of decision, the best thing you can do is the right thing, the next best thing is the wrong thing, and the worst thing you can do is nothing." – **Teddy Roosevelt**

Chapter 12 – Optimizer

An "optimizer" is someone who is not happy with the status quo and who wants to make things operate in a smoother and more efficient manner. It's very important for every business owner or manager to have this characteristic when running an organization and to bring people into the organization that also recognize its importance.

Optimizers are constantly evaluating every portion of their personal and professional lives in hopes of making things better. Sometimes these people can be maddening because they never seem to be satisfied and they are always tinkering with how things are done. You may be married to an optimizer because they are always moving things around in the kitchen and straightening out the junk drawer. They continually want to make things more organized in the house, and while they are at work they are always focused on devising a new way to make a business process more effective. Thankfully, these people exist because they will help you streamline your business processes and ultimately make you more effective. This is also a characteristic that virtually anyone with the right type of desire can learn. Business owners or managers need to be a part of these optimizing activities and need to display the drive and determination to ensure that these optimization programs are implemented effectively.

Personal organization is the first step in being a good optimizer. How can you fix other situations or help other people if you are a disorganized mess? The answer is that you can't.

The first aspect of becoming a good optimizer is focusing on how you can develop your individual organizational skills.

Individual organizational skills

We have all probably walked into a business and some people in a department appear overwhelmed while others seem calm and in control. But what makes one person seem organized and able to handle multiple priorities with ease, while another person seem like they are running around like a chicken with their head cut off? Some of it can simply be attributed to the type of person they are, but most of it goes back to how organized the person is on a day-to-day basis. The calm person will have implemented some sort of organizational program that they have either been taught or that they learned themselves, while the other person is left scratching their head wondering where all of the hours in the day went.

Here's a list of **15 Tips for Better Organization** that will help you be more efficient on an individual basis if you do not already have a program in place:

1. **Organize your workspace** – Clear your desk from as much clutter as possible and file things in an orderly fashion so that you can retrieve them when appropriate. Set an internal goal to only handle pieces of paper one time and one time only. Do this as much as possible for emails as well... Read them and deal with them.
2. **Create a welcoming environment** – Clearing your desk of clutter is one thing, but creating a work environment that you find appealing will make you feel more comfortable, make it easier for you to focus on the task at hand, and help to alleviate some of the stress that you may feel daily. You may want to consider using alternative types of lighting or having pictures of loved ones on your desk. Anything that will make you feel more comfortable will help.
3. **To-Do list** – Make a to-do list and prioritize each one placing the most important AND urgent item first and working down from there. Carry it with you at ALL times

and be diligent about utilizing it as a tool. Given that you will constantly be adding and modifying the items on the list I would suggest that you use some sort of electronic media, but you can also use a manual method if you prefer. Remember to review what you've done at the end of each day and make a new list or modify the existing one for the next day.

4. **The ABC method** - Ensure that what you think is important is really important and what is urgent is really urgent. Not every important item is urgent so you may have to focus on urgent, yet less important issues throughout the day. Use the following method to help prioritize your list:

> **"A" or "High"** – Items that are important and urgent

> **"B" or "Medium"** – Items that are important but not urgent

> **"C" or "Low"** – Items that are neither important nor urgent.

5. **Create an activity Log** – It's critical that you take at least one week to honestly log your activity and the time you spend on each item during your work day. Since this will be a private list that only you will see you need to keep track of business and personal items such as surfing the Internet, taking personal phone calls, or hanging around the water cooler. Everyone needs some free time during the day, but you may be surprised at how much time you spend on non-work related activities. This log will help you recognize if you are spending your time on high value items or simple distractions that can easily be put off until a later time or ignored altogether. If the majority of your time is being spent on high value items and you are overwhelmed

then you may have to work on your ability and willingness to delegate.

6. **Identify time limits** – For every item on your to-do list, identify the amount of time you feel it will take in order to complete the task. Remember that your goal is to be able to complete your business related tasks within your regularly scheduled work day. Allocating a certain amount of time for each event will help you determine if you are heading towards a problem or if things are on track for completion. Try to stick to the times you have allocated as much as possible. If you are constantly underestimating how much time you need to complete a task then add additional time until your accuracy improves. Over time every conscientious person will get better at this.

7. **Email** - Deal with E-mail at set times of the day if it is appropriate. This may not be possible for everyone in an organization, but try to limit your "ad-hoc" sessions to no more than five minutes.

8. **Use only one calendar** – Create one calendar (hopefully, in an electronic format) and use it for all of your activities. Even private matters can be added to a tool like Outlook and marked as private. This will keep others from seeing the details, but it will allow them to see that you will be busy during certain hours. It will also provide you some peace of mind by not having to manage multiple calendars.

9. **Schedule uninterrupted time** - Schedule some uninterrupted time every day that will allow you to focus on important and urgent tasks. Obviously, the amount of time you schedule will vary given the items on your list. If you're using a version of Microsoft Outlook put it on your shared calendar so that others will see that you are unavailable during specific times.

10. **One bite at a time** – *How do you eat a six ton elephant? One bite at a time.* Large, complex problems or tasks can easily seem overwhelming. Cut these big jobs into

small, more manageable chunks. Prioritize each chunk by the time, importance and urgency that they will require and work on one chunk at a time. Remember to schedule some extra time to complete the overall project as unexpected events may arise that will slow things down. Building some wiggle room into the project will also help alleviate some stress.

11. **Automate when possible** – Technology changes at an incredible pace. Quite frequently, new and quicker ways of doing things exist that we may not even be aware of especially if we are overwhelmed and focused on the immediate tasks with which we are challenged. We often do not think that there might be a better or easier way to perform a repetitive task. Ask your supervisor or IT team if they are aware of any new technology that can help perform these types of tasks in a quicker and more efficient way. You may be surprised and quite thankful in what you find!

12. **Delegate** – If you're leading a team working on a project don't forget to delegate specific responsibilities to the other members and hold them accountable in an appropriate fashion. New supervisors or team leaders often feel that they have to do the tasks themselves if they want it done correctly. This is a sure fire way to meet with disaster and it must be avoided at all costs. Make the assignments clear, establish firm deadlines and have meetings or discussions frequently to ensure that your team is on track for a successful completion.

13. **Don't over commit** – We all have deadlines that we must meet, but it is important that you be honest with yourself by not over-committing to an activity. If someone asks to get involved in a new task or project make sure that you can actually complete it in the time allocated. If not, you will be doing everyone, including yourself, a disservice. As a business owner it is your responsibility to determine what you can accomplish and what you can't, but if you are not the owner of the

company then always discuss the details and timeframe with your supervisor. Share the other items on your list so they can see everything else that you are expected to accomplish. A good supervisor will understand this and help you re-prioritize your list if necessary.

14. **Communicate** – Make sure that you keep the lines of communication open to your team members and that they know that open and honest dialogue is a necessity in building a strong business. Your team wants to accomplish their tasks, but sometimes too many things get piled upon their plates. It is important that they know that they will not be chastised by identifying any issues they may be having. They must understand and accept that it is much better for everyone to discuss problems BEFORE the expected deadline arrives and not after.

If people on your team have a lot of tasks on their list then schedule a meeting with them each week to review the items and come to some agreement on priorities and perhaps new deadlines. Make sure they know that they should not be afraid to ask for help when they need it!

15. **An on-going process** – Realize that your organizing skills and ability will get better the longer you practice and implement them. Organizing yourself and your team members is not a destination, it is a journey. It is a never-ending process that you and every member of your team need to sharpen and hone until it becomes second nature.

Other tools for individual organization

There are a number of viable solutions available in the market to help get you organized. I am not recommending any particular product, but many of you are probably already aware of one of the most popular, and manual, tools from a company called Day-

Timer. They offer a myriad of paper based options for getting control over your life. Although I am not a fan of doing this type of activity by hand many people still find it to be quite effective.

Most businesses use Microsoft products including Outlook and Exchange as their email applications. Outlook also provides tools that can easily be used to keep track not only of your email and calendar, but also your prioritized task list. Mobile applications allow it to synchronize the data with your phone or tablet device which gives you the flexibility of having your task list in an electronic and very portable format.

Microsoft also has OneNote, a note taking tool that many people find quite useful. There are countless other third party software applications that are available if a manual based system or the basic tools in Outlook are not appropriate for your situation. A quick Google search for *organizing software* shows 36,000,000 results... happy hunting!

As a manager you may want to offer a class on organizational skills that you can either teach yourself or bring in a third party consultant for a brief seminar. I typically like to do these types of things myself, but sometimes people pay more attention to the message when it is delivered by a third party.

No matter what solution you choose, it is important for you as a business owner/manager to use some sort of time management tool and to help train your employees to use that solution as well. It will help you and your company to be more efficient and to complete your daily work with a lot less stress.

Business process optimization

Optimizing things related to your personal business situation is very important, but fixing, or optimizing the other aspects of your business in general encompasses more that keeping a tidy desk and staying on top of planned activities and tasks. Successfully optimizing your business means evaluating all of your internal processes and continuously tweaking them.

One way that this can easily be done is by implementing the concept of Kaizen throughout your organization. The Japanese refer to this process of continuous improvement as Kaizen with "Kai" meaning change and "Zen" meaning good. Thus, change for the good or improvement.

Wikipedia provides a nice overview of the Japanese idea of Kaizen which follows:

> "Kaizen is a daily process, the purpose of which goes beyond simple productivity improvement. It is also a process that, when done correctly, humanizes the workplace, eliminates overly hard work ("muri"), and teaches people how to perform experiments on their work using the scientific method and how to learn to spot and eliminate waste in business processes.
>
> In all, the process suggests a humanized approach to workers and to increasing productivity: "The idea is to nurture the company's human resources as much as it is to praise and encourage participation in kaizen activities." Successful implementation requires "the participation of workers in the improvement." People at all levels of an organization participate in kaizen, from the CEO down to janitorial staff, as well as external stakeholders when applicable.
>
> The format for kaizen can be individual, suggestion system, small group, or large group. At Toyota, it is usually a local improvement within a workstation or local area and involves a small group in improving their own work environment and productivity. This group is often guided through the kaizen process by a line supervisor; sometimes this is the line supervisor's key role. Kaizen

on a broad, cross-departmental scale in companies, generates total quality management, and frees human efforts through improving productivity using machines and computing power.

While kaizen (at Toyota) usually delivers small improvements, the culture of continual aligned small improvements and standardization yields large results in terms of overall improvement in productivity. This philosophy differs from the "command and control" improvement programs of the mid-twentieth century. Kaizen methodology includes making changes and monitoring results, then adjusting. Large-scale pre-planning and extensive project scheduling are replaced by smaller experiments, which can be rapidly adapted as new improvements are suggested. "

Everyone must recognize the importance of this type of activity whether or not it is called Kaizen, TQM, Six Sigma, or any other of the more popular names often used throughout the industrialized world. The processes may vary slightly, but the end goal to deliver small improvements on a continual basis remains identical.

As an outline, there are a number of standards steps for implementing a continuous improvement program that are all part of organizing yourself and your team:

1. Define and document the current situation and problems
2. Discuss and create a vision of how things would be in an ideal situation
3. Set up clearly defined and measurable targets
4. Assemble a team of people with experience in the area you wish to improve and brainstorm solutions to the problem
5. Develop a detailed "Kaizen" plan that will clearly define the steps to be taken

6. After implementation measure your results to your defined targets
7. Prepare summary documents and standard operating procedures based upon the improvements you have implemented.
8. Create a program of on-going evaluation that will help your continuous improvement program

Another aspect of Kaizen is often called the "**5S" Methodology** and it is frequently attributed to either Hiroyuki Hirano or Takashi Osada:

1. **Sort** – identify and remove unnecessary items. Evaluate necessary items to see if they can be sourced less expensively.
2. **Straighten or streamline** – Arrange necessary items in a logical order so that they can be easily found when needed. Prevent wasted time and ensure that things are handled on a first come first served basis.
3. **Shine** – Ensure that your workplace has been cleaned and inspected which will help prevent machine and or equipment deterioration.
4. **Standardize** – Maintain high standards of workplace organization and housekeeping at all times.
5. **Sustain** – Keep the continuous improvement program in an on-going fashion. Don't be satisfied with the latest improvements and keep looking for more.

Unfortunately, in many work environments a departmental manager may not know how their employees handle their daily workload. If you ask one of these supervisors if they can better organize the daily activity of their teammates you will often get an answer that they have not had the chance to really evaluate the situation in detail.

Because of this, it is important to ask yourself and your team to think about the work that they do and to come up with suggestions on how things might be better. Some simple questions to ask might be:

- Is there any work being done in my department that is really not necessary or completely redundant?
- Can any of the work that is currently being done be simplified in any way?
- Can any of my staff come up with a better way of doing their assigned tasks
- What will be the result if we change?

An example of wasted work comes to us by Masao Nemoto the former Managing Director of Toyota Motor Corporation:

> *"An employee in an office had the responsibility to transcribe the contents of payment vouchers and receiving slips into a notebook. The worker said "I inherited this work from my predecessor. I have been on this job for two years and no one has ever asked to see the notebook. If I stop doing this work, I can save 20 hours each month." In suggesting that this work be eliminated, she also mentioned that all the chits were kept in the document room, and any necessary information could be obtained within 30 minutes. If the work had not been utilized for two years, there was certainly no justification for the continuation, especially when there was another way of finding the required information."*

How many situations like the one above exist in organizations throughout the world?   How many go uncovered year after year? How much more productive and profitable can an organization be if they take the steps to fix these types of situations?

Kaizen success examples in business

Canon - Canon of Japan wanted to overcome international competition and expand its operations on a global scale. The management team developed a matrix management system with a variety of small group activities. The purpose was to reinvigorate their workforce, improve their overall business processes and finally to eliminate waste. Techniques like Canon Production System, Quality Assurance, Production Assurance, and Personnel Training were developed and introduced and Canon was able to achieve a world class 3% per month productivity increase.

Gold Seal Engineering Products - is an India based spares parts manufacturer for the automotive industry. The 5S principles of Kaizen were implemented which cut down on their production set-up time by 33%. Additionally, in 6 months their lead time was down by 25%, scrap was reduced by 75%, machine down time dropped by 60%, and response time got reduced by 42%.

An anonymous US factory

Michael Baudin has been a consultant since 1987 and provides the following example of Kaizen at work in a US factory:

> *The picture below shows a work piece in the vise that is 28 feet long and requires greasing in multiple locations. The operator on the left was tired of running back and forth to a fixed location to pick up the grease. The cart now contains everything he needs to apply grease anywhere on the work piece, and he wheels it back and forth as needed. To the right is the production supervisor for the area, who supports this and other similar projects.*

How was it actually done? The production team from this area was given a budget of $500/operator to spend as they saw fit on supplies and devices for improvement projects at a Home Depot store. Their actual spend worked out to $113/operator, including the cart and bins you see on the picture and a magnetic sweeper.

It is a perfect illustration of the Kaizen concept. It is too small an improvement to warrant the attention of engineers or managers, yet it makes the work easier for the operator and makes him more productive.

An individual success story

The open source six sigma website called treQna.com published a blog outlining how one person gained control over their work life through the effective use of time management skills/tools. A slightly modified summary of that blog follows:

> *I recently spent coaching time with a client that had many concerns regarding his personal productivity. Like many people these days, he wears many different job function hats and he performs all or part of what in previous times, would have been the duties of additional people within his organization.*
>
> *This individual was very frustrated that he couldn't seem to get much done during his work day and found the need to extend his hours just to complete his daily assignments. For the past several months he had been working more than 60 hours each week just to stay even with his duties. The stress of these long hours and the pressures from home were adding to his frustration and he was seriously considering seeking employment elsewhere.*
>
> *We took some time to discuss his typical work day and how he managed his many activities, most of which to him always seemed to be urgent. He already had a time management software tool but he was not using it for its' intended purpose. After a little while I was able to convince him to diligently follow the prescribed methodologies contained in the software and the results were impressive.*
>
> *After a few weeks he now reports that his frustration levels have dropped considerably, he gets along much better with his work associates, and he accomplishes more of the truly important tasks on-time and with much*

less stress. He also reports his work hours are quickly slipping back into 40 per week and he was amazed that something as simple as using time management tools could so easily resolve so much of his frustration.

His team is also now more productive and happier as a result. His boss is more understanding and cooperative, and the entire management team is now using this time management software as well. All in all a pretty good result!

Kaizen or continuous improvement is a wonderful process to implement and follow at any organization. It can be time consuming and quite detailed work, especially if you want to do it correctly. You need to be committed to the task and you may find that many in your organization will complain that it will be a waste of time. Please keep this in mind as you undertake this process, because it will be your drive, commitment, and competitive spirit that will get the program of the ground and keep it on track.

You may want to go slowly at first and concentrate on one department at a time. This will give you some idea as to the effort and time you will have to allocate as you go forward. It will definitely be a worthwhile investment as your business will begin to operate in a more efficient manner, people will have less stress, and your overall profitability will increase.

Management Checklist:

- ✓ Do I have my own organizational process that I utilize each day? Am I a good role model?
- ✓ Do I convey to my team the importance of being organized and implementing an improvement program?
- ✓ Have I created an environment in which people feel comfortable conveying the truth about their individual

situation and when they may be falling behind on their tasks?
- ✓ Have I provided my team members with the correct tools in order to successfully organize their work environment?
- ✓ Have I evaluated each business process in order to organize, improve and streamline each area?
- ✓ Am I open to suggestions from my team on better ways to organize different aspects of the business?

"Excellent firms don't believe in excellence - only in constant improvement and constant change." – **Tom Peters**

"Clutter is the physical manifestation of unmade decisions fueled by procrastination" - **Christina Scalise**

"Good order is the foundation of all things" - **Edmund Burke**

Chapter 13 - Creativity

The Creativity Blog posted the following statement:

> *"Creativity is the act of turning new and imaginative ideas into reality. Creativity is characterized by the ability to perceive the world in new ways, to find hidden patterns, to make connections between seemingly unrelated phenomena, and to generate solutions. Creativity involves two processes: thinking, then producing. If you have ideas, but don't act on them, you are imaginative but not creative."*

The last sentence above is something key to remember. Creativity *and your ability to act* is a must for members of any organization that wants to be successful and remain successful over the long run. Even if you have an outstanding product right now that is selling like hot cakes you will still need to develop it further or create a replacement product if you want to remain competitive in the future. Your competitors are not stupid, they see what you are offering and they are asking their most creative people to come up with a better version of what you are offering. This is what competition and capitalism is all about.

Preston Waters stated the following in an article published on elitedaily.com that sums up the importance of creativity for the business world:

> *"In today's business world the only way to separate yourself from the rest is not with your fancy resume that you printed at Kinkos, or your GPA that you basically overdosed on Adderall in order to attain. It is how well you can think for yourself and actually use your creativity that separates you from everyone else.*

When most people out there see a problem, they just complain about it instead of trying to resolve it because they never had to use their creativity to problem shoot before.

We live in a world that is constantly becoming innovated with new concepts, ideas and technology. Having the creativity to help innovate something that has never been created before- anything from a product to a piece of art- is all based on where your mind wants to take you. But so many never even allow their mind to journey out of their cubicle, but instead get stuck in that cubicle for the rest of their lives.

People in today's world need to realize that individuals in leadership positions must be creative and become creative problem solvers as these are skills of the future. You need to unleash your creativity and understand how important it truly is to have it flourish throughout your life and career.

> *"Creativity is more than just being different. Anybody can plan weird; that's easy. What's hard is to be as simple as Bach. Making the simple, awesomely simple, that's creativity" – Charles Mingus*

Many times in today's world there is little time to no time allocated towards real thinking and brainstorming, or even experimentation without judgment. With so much pressure to produce quick results in the current economic environment, it may seem like a luxury to walk away from the mountain of tasks to be accomplished.

What you need to understand is that your creativity is what makes your life fun and is what gets you excited each and every day you wake up in the morning."

Set expectations

As a business owner you can set an example by bringing creative practices and theories to your business. Hiring people that have a creative streak will pay huge dividends to every organization. You need people that are constantly looking at situations and trying to figure out what can be done better and faster on a continual basis.

Applying creativity to business situations means that many things can and will probably change on a relatively frequent basis. It is your job as an owner or manager to get your team to realize that this type of "change" is healthy for a business and to embrace the entire process.

Gerald Puccio department chairman and professor at the International Center for Studies in Creativity at Buffalo State College stated the following that illustrates the point:

> "Given the pace of change, organizations rise and fall faster than ever before; witness Blockbuster, Nokia and Motorola. So how does an organization survive in such tumultuous times? The same way humans have survived throughout history."

Puccio suggests that organizations use collective imagination to develop solutions to evolving challenges because imaginative responses are much more likely to sustain innovation. Without creative thinking, organizations miss out on breakthrough ideas that can become innovations.

Creativity success stories

At one of my previous companies a major part of our business was selling consumable products to industrial laboratories throughout the US and Canada. For many years sales were won on who could provide these consumables (that were considered to be commodity items) in the cheapest fashion. We were in a constant battle with mom and pop type organizations that had little overhead and who would continuously undercut our prices in order to steal our business. In this type of environment maintaining long term customers is quite difficult and the motivation of our sales team often suffered.

Thankfully, a team of very creative people at the parent company in Copenhagen, Denmark came up with an idea on how to re-invent the technology, raising an entire product line from being a commodity to a unique, better, and yes more expensive product. Not surprisingly, it immediately began to dominate the market and profits flourished. At first our competitors created every excuse known to man in order to convince people that our new technology would not work, but they quickly realized that they were fighting a losing battle. Soon, they all started to try and duplicate our solution with minor technological differences. Thankfully, we had created a position in the market that allowed our dominance for over five years.

Perhaps the most important example of creativity was demonstrated by Tim Berners-Lee and Robert Cailliau who in 1990 developed a hypertext product called the World Wide Web (WWW). Many people believe that this was the beginning of the internet, but this is incorrect as the Internet was actually created in 1969 by members of ARPANET. For 21 years the Internet existed in obscurity and it was typically only used by highly technical people. It was the vision and creativity of Lee and Cailliau who recognized what "might be" and put the tools in place that gave us this wonderful tool that we now all use every day. Imagine what our world would be like if these two individuals did not have the creative genius to make this existing tool more user friendly.

Fostering creativity with your business

How can a manager foster creativity within their organization?

It should be no surprise that numerous studies have been done over the years which can lead to a myriad of suggestions depending upon what journal you read. One that I found quite interesting was published by the *Harvard Business Review*. They cited a study from Professor Teresa Amabile, the text of which follows:

> *"The words creativity and innovation tend to be used interchangeably, but when it comes to novel ideas in business, they are not necessarily the same thing.*
>
> *"Creativity and innovation are different stages in the same process," says Professor Teresa M. Amabile. "Creativity is the initial production and development of novel, useful ideas. Innovation is the successful implementation of creative ideas." In other words, she says, creativity is the "front end" of the process, while innovation is the "back-end" result.*
>
> *With degrees in chemistry and psychology, Amabile has spent more than three decades exploring how work environments can help or hinder the creative process. What she has found is that while the fruits of innovation are often in plain view, the seeds of creativity are much harder to spot—occurring deep inside what she calls the "inner work life" of employees.*
>
> *"Creativity requires very high levels of intrinsic motivation," she says—that is, it has much more to do with an employee's inner passion for doing great work than any outside motivators like incentives.*
>
> *In an effort to better understand exactly where that motivation comes from, Amabile spearheaded a study of more than 200 knowledge workers over a three-year period, asking them to keep journal entries of their successes and frustrations at work. What she found was*

unexpected: It wasn't recognition or awards that most ignited employees and freed up their creative juices. Rather, employees tended to be most engaged by regular, incremental progress toward the accomplishment of a meaningful goal—a phenomenon Amabile calls The Progress Principle, which is also the title of her new book.

Analyzing some 12,000 journal entries, Amabile consistently found that these so-called small wins were more frequently associated with the positive emotions and intrinsic motivation that in turn generated the creativity needed to develop innovative approaches to problems. That doesn't mean that managers don't have some control over the internal processes of their employees' minds—quite the contrary. "As a manager of people, you should regard this as very good news," Amabile wrote in the Harvard Business Review. "The key to motivation turns out to be largely within your control."

By setting clear, achievable goals, allowing autonomy in achieving those goals, and removing distractions or unnecessary time pressures, managers can help free up employees' creative impulses and guide them down the path of real innovations that can help the company.

"In contrast to the creative process, the innovation process can happen when people are in a more extrinsically motivated state, focusing on the deadline, the profitability goals," she says. "Ideally, they will still be passionate about the work, but it's important at that point to focus in and to make sure the details of implementation are right.""

Her statement that creativity requires high levels of intrinsic motivation was no surprise to me. This is why it is so important to find people who have demonstrated this type of behavior in the past and to bring them into your organization.

What surprises me is not that recognition and rewards have little to do with the creative process, but that it is the "small wins" that motivate people and stir the creative process. Perhaps it will give a slightly new insight into creating an environment that will foster and develop more creativity.

Stanford University listed five important things to remember regarding creativity in an online course on the subject:

1. Creativity is essential for leadership, happiness and success.
2. Everyone is creative – you don't have to be an artist!
3. Creativity is often blocked by fear, judgment and the inner critic
4. Paying attention to creativity brings it out.
5. Creativity is idiosyncratic – we each have our own gifts, experiences, and talents.

Boost your creativity

Gregory Ciotti posted an article on Lifehacker entitled "Nine of the Best Ways To Boost Creative Thinking" which further develops the concept. I have summarized it below with some slight modifications:

1. **Restrict Yourself** - Research shows that many people often take the path of "least mental resistance," building on ideas they already have or trying to use *every* resource at hand. The thing is, the research also suggests that placing self-imposed limitations can boost creativity because it forces even creative people to work outside of their comfort zones. One of the most famous examples is when Dr. Seuss produced Green Eggs & Ham after a bet where he was challenged by his editor to produce an entire book in less than 50 different words.

Try limiting your work in some way and you may see the benefits of your brain coming up with creative solutions to finish a project around the parameters you've set.

2. **Re-Conceptualize the Problem** - One thing that researchers have noticed with especially creative people is that they tend to re-conceptualize the problem more often than their less creative counterparts. That means, instead of thinking of a cut-and-dry end goal to certain situations, they sit back and examine the problem in different ways before beginning to work. A writer who handles content strategy for startups may set a "cookie cutter" goal to "write popular articles." The problem is, if he/she approaches an article with the mindset of, "What can I write that will get a lot of tweets?" they often will not come up with something very good. However, if they step back and examine the problem from another angle, such as: "What sort of articles really resonate with people and capture their interest?" then they are focusing on a far better fundamental part of the problem, and they will achieve their other goals by coming up with something more original. So, if you find yourself stagnating by focusing on generic problems like "What would be something cool to paint?" try to re-conceptualize the problem by focusing on a more meaningful angle such as "What sort of painting evokes the feeling of loneliness that we all encounter after a break-up?"

3. **Create Psychological Distance** - It's long been known that abstaining from a task is useful for breaking through a creative block, and it also seems that creating "psychological" distance may also be useful. Subjects in a recent study were able to solve twice as many insight problems when asked to think about the source of the task as distant, rather than it being close in proximity. Try to imagine your creative task as being disconnected and distant from your current position or location. According to this research, this may make the problem

more accessible and can encourage higher level thinking.

4. **Daydream… but do your work first!** - Although study after study confirms that daydreaming and napping can help with the creative thought process, there is one piece of research that everybody seems to leave out. One study in particular shows that the less work you've done on a problem, the less daydreaming will help you. That is, daydreaming and incubation are most effective on a project you've already invested a lot of creative effort into. So before you try to use naps and daydreams as an excuse for not working, be honest with yourself and don't forget to hustle first!

5. **Embrace Something Absurd** - Research suggests that reading or experiencing something absurd or surreal can help boost pattern recognition and creative thinking. Subjects in the study read Franz Kafka, but even stories like Alice in Wonderland have been suggested by psychologists. The conclusion was that the mind is always seeking to make sense of the things that it sees, and surreal, absurd art puts the mind in "overdrive" for a short period while it tries to work out just exactly what it is looking at or reading.

6. **Separate Work from Consumption** - Also known as the "absorb state," this technique has been shown to help with the incubation process and is far more effective than trying to combine work with creative thinking. It makes sense too—we are often in two very different states of mind when absorbing an activity and when we are trying to create something. One author found that their writing broke down when they tried to handle research and writing at the same time, and are much better off when they just turn off their "work mode" and consume more inspiration in the form of reading, watching, and observing.

7. **Create During a Powerful Mood** - For a long time, the research has pointed to happiness as being the ideal

state to create in. Recently though, a relatively new study on creativity in the workplace made this bold conclusion: Creativity increased when both positive and negative emotions were running high. The implication seems to be that while certain negative moods can be creativity killers, they aren't as universal as positive moods (joy, being excited, love, etc) in that sometimes they may spur creative thinking rather than hinder it. Please don't try to put yourself in a bad mood to create something, but next time you're in a strong emotional state, try to sit down and focus that energy on creating something and you may be surprised by the end result.

8. **Get Moving** - Is there any wonder that 'exercising more" is one of the most desired good habits in the entire world? Some research even suggests that exercise can actually boost creative thinking as well, due to its' ability to get the heart pumping and put people in a positive mood. It's similar to how other research shows that thinking about love can produce more creative thoughts; it's not necessarily the act, it's the change in mood. If you're stuck in a creative rut and want to take a break, try including exercise while your brain is subconsciously at work, it may help to speed up your "Aha!" moment.

9. **Ask, "What Might Have Been?"** - According to the research surrounding the process of counterfactual thinking, looking at a situation that has already occurred and asking yourself, "What could have happened?" can boost creativity for short periods of time.

These are simply suggestions for what have worked for other people. What works for you or the people around you may be entirely different. The important thing is to continually try and develop your creativity and to surround yourself with people that have demonstrated creativity AND the ability to take action.

Creativity in business

A survey was completed by IBM in which they asked 1,500 CEO's to list the most important leadership characteristics and "creativity" was the highest ranked item on their list. I'm not sure I completely agree with this sentiment, but I certainly concur that creativity is extremely important.

Google has been one of the most talked about and successful companies since it went public in 2004. Many organizations now try to emulate how Google's does things and the search giant is certainly considered to have one of the most creative teams of people assembled in a corporate environment. This is by design and Google spends a lot of time trying to uncover these people during the interview process. Nicholas Carlson from *Business Insider* published the following list of 15 interview questions that are reportedly used at Google in order to determine how creative a person might be:

1. *How many golf balls can fit in a school bus?*
2. *How much should you charge to wash all of the windows in Seattle?*
3. *In a country in which people only want boys, every family continues to have children until they have a boy. If they have a girl, they have another child. If they have a boy, they stop. What is the proportion of boys to girls in the country?*
4. *How many piano tuners are there in the entire world?*
5. *Why are manhole covers round?*
6. *Design an evacuation plan for San Francisco.*
7. *How many times a day do the hands of a clock overlap?*
8. *Explain the significance of dead beef.*
9. *A man pushed his car into a hotel and lost his fortune. What happened?*

10. You need to check that your friend, Bob, has your correct phone number, but you cannot ask him directly. You must write the question on a card and give it to Eve who will take the card to Bob and return the answer to you. What must you write on the card, besides the question, to ensure Bob can encode the message so that Eve cannot read your phone number?

11. You're the captain of a pirate ship, and your crew gets to vote on how the gold is divided up. If fewer than half of the pirates agree with you, you die. How do you recommend apportioning the gold in such a way that you get a good share of the booty, but still survive?

12. You have eight balls all of the same size, 7 of them weigh the same, and one of them weighs slightly more. How can you find the ball that is heavier by using a balance and only two weighings?

13. You are given 2 eggs and you have access to a 100-story building. The eggs you have been given can be very hard or very fragile meaning that they may break if dropped from the first floor or may not even break if dropped from 100th floor. Both types of eggs are identical in appearance. You need to figure out the highest floor of a 100-story building an egg can be dropped without breaking. The question is how many drops you need to make. You are allowed to break 2 eggs in the process.

14. Explain a database in three sentences to your eight-year-old nephew.

15. You are shrunk to the height of a nickel and your mass is proportionally reduced so as to maintain your original density. You are then thrown into an empty glass blender. The blades will start moving in 60 seconds. What do you do?

I'm not sure that I can answer too many of these questions in an intelligent fashion, but I thought it might be interesting to share them with you nonetheless. Google wouldn't go through these steps if they were not focused on hiring extremely creative people. Perhaps these types of people will not even take the time to apply to your organization, but you can easily take your own steps to try and hire people that will bring a creative passion to your business nonetheless. Use some of these questions from Google or come up with some of your own, but make finding creative people part of your hiring process. It will most assuredly benefit your entire business.

Be creative. Be successful. Be great!

Management Checklist

- ✓ Am I the type of manager that is constantly seeking out new and innovative ways of doing things, or am I more interested in maintaining the status quo.
- ✓ Have I created an environment that fosters creative ideas among my teammates?
- ✓ Do I actively seek out creative people when adding members to my team?
- ✓ What was the last truly creative thing that I have contributed to the organization? If you can't think of one then you are not applying your creativity to your role in the organization.
- ✓ Do I allow for brainstorming sessions for teams in the office to uncover better and more creative ways of doing things?

"Around here, however, we don't look backwards for very long. We keep moving forward, opening up new doors and doing new things, because we're curious...and curiosity keeps leading us down new paths." - **Walt Disney Company**

"Others have seen what is and asked why. I have seen what could be and asked why not. " – **Pablo Picasso**

"I never made one of my discoveries through the process of rational thinking" — **Albert Einstein**

Chapter 14 - Initiative

Most successful people do not wait around to be told what to do. People that wait around to be told what to do are not "do-ers" or leaders, they are followers. As a leader you need to demonstrate initiative every day. You set the table for the entire organization and if your people see you utilizing your creativity and taking the initiative to fix problems then they will begin to do so as well. Buying and reading this book was a simple act of initiative. Starting your business, or applying for a management role, were huge acts of initiative. I am sure they are just a few examples of what got you to where you are today, but you must continually display this trait on a daily basis if you want to build a long term, successful organization.

It is also important to create an environment that welcomes initiative and encourages people to act with confidence and independence. Giving people on your team the ability to demonstrate initiative often takes a lot of courage because sometimes things may not turn out as expected. It's imperative that business owners and managers work through these situations in a positive fashion. If things did not turn out well then sit down with the person who took the initiative and discuss the situation with them. Find out why they took the actions they did and coach them on what they might have done differently. Whatever you do, don't verbally beat them up or berate them. If you do, you will most probably never see an act of initiative from that person again. This would most certainly be a mistake!

Sometimes the negative consequence of a poorly considered initiative will cause knee jerk reactions by managers that stifle independent, creative thinking.   If you ever get to the point where you tell your people to "just do what I tell you and nothing else" then all you have done is crush everyone's initiative. Confident, thoughtful people will never flourish in this type of environment, nor will they feel fulfilled while working under such a manager. You must either change your behavior or risk hurting your organization and your long term viability.

Early in my career I experienced this attitude first hand. After a few months in a new position I became aware that the POS System we were using offered remote printers that could immediately print what was input at the terminal used by the servers and bartenders into the kitchen. This would enable servers to stay on the floor with their customers rather than walking back to the kitchen with a paper copy of an order each time someone wanted to purchase food. To me this seemed like a brilliant idea and so I took it to my supervisor.

Now, my boss was a great guy. He was very friendly and fair to everyone. The only negative thing about him was that he was extremely risk averse. In fact, he was so risk averse that he immediately said no to my idea. When I asked him why he would not pursue the idea the only answer he was able to give me was that "it is not the way we do things". I indicated that I understood, but I asked him why we couldn't change the way we do things? Of course, his response was "because that's not the way we do things!"

Today, these types of remote printers sitting in kitchens and bars are ubiquitous, but his refusal to seriously explore it as an option taught me an important lesson on how a lack of creativity and inability to take any risk whatsoever could potentially hurt a business.

In my opinion, the POS system we were utilizing was not very user friendly and seemed to break down too often, so I asked my boss if I could start looking for a replacement. I think he just wanted to give me something to do to keep me quiet so he said yes. I began to review the available options in the market and after a short time I recommended that we purchase a new system from a large, international computer and POS company. Amazingly, the upper management agreed with my proposal, and we began to install these new systems throughout our organization. One thing to note is that they utilized remote printers in the kitchen and at the bar. I am pleased to say that they were a huge success! I'm glad I wasn't deterred by my boss's attitude and lack of creativity.

No matter how great a manager you may be, you will never be able to plan in advance for every situation that may arise. In order to meet these challenges you need people that can think on their feet and devise solutions to their problems that will help grow your business. You do not need robots or automatons that blindly follow orders regardless of the circumstances. The business world does not operate in such a fashion and you should not expect this from your team members.

I have run numerous organizations and I always wanted to surround myself with people that took the initiative to recognize and fix problems without having to be told. I never want people around me that would wait for me to tell them what I wanted them to do next. If I had been clear in painting a picture of how I wanted our organization to run, with an emphasis on the principles that are important to success, then most of the time intelligent people using their own initiative will be able empowered to make the right decisions.

On occasion, people will make mistakes, but I never faulted someone for trying to make things right. If something was handled poorly, I would talk about the situation afterward and explain how their course of action might have been improved. It is in every business owner's best interest to hire smart people and to give them the freedom to use that intelligence to help make your business better.

Lessons learned

During WWII the allied forces launched one of the largest naval assaults in the history of humanity on the beaches of France. During the D-Day landing the front line commanders of the

German forces were not allowed to make any decisions on how to stymie the attack. The rigid line of command was so ingrained that they felt powerless to make their own decisions. It was so bad that no commands were given for many hours because no one had the guts to wake the Fuhrer and give him the bad news. Thankfully, this type of mindless adherence to rigid communication lines allowed the allies to take control of the beaches and begin the end of the war in Europe.

Policy manuals are a great tool because they give a detailed guideline on expectations and how things should be run in an organization. But, (and this is a big but) policy manuals cannot foresee every situation that a manager will face. Successful businesses need people that can think and apply logic and sound business practices to the situations they encounter. If all we had to do was look at a policy manual to determine the best course of action, then we would not need managers. We all know that this is not the case and thus the reason why you need people that show initiative coupled with sound judgment and creativity.

Early on in my career I was the marketing director at a small organization that had just started using a CRM tool. I knew nothing about CRM at the time so I started to play around with the system. I took note of how it was set up and I saw a lot of short comings in the programming. I went to my boss and told her that I thought we could update the system with a little effort so that we would have a much better sales and management tool. She thanked me for letting her know my thoughts, but she told me that it was not necessary because our sales manager loved the system as it was. She clearly indicated that it was all that our organization needed and that I should not waste my time by customizing it any further.

I left her office a bit perplexed, but nevertheless undaunted. After a week or so, I took a laptop home and in the evening hours I re-programmed the system to what I thought was a better way of doing things. After a few weeks of work I had finally completed the metamorphosis and I somewhat hesitantly asked my boss to allow me to demonstrate how the new system could work.

I had taken a huge risk, but thankfully my boss was very open-minded and immediately saw the benefits of the new system that I had created. Within a few weeks, she flew me to the worldwide headquarters in Copenhagen, Denmark so that I could show the owners and they were equally impressed. We soon began to use this new system in the US and at other sites throughout our international organization. Looking back I now recognize that this was one of the earliest acts of impactful initiative and creativity that I had taken. It certainly put me in a bright spotlight and it allowed others much higher up in the organization to see me in a very positive light.

Please know that allowing people to use their own initiative is not a licensed free for all. I am not espousing that you create a situation in which any person, can make any decision, at any time, with no consequences. That would be ludicrous. What I am suggesting is letting people in your organization evaluate their situation and to make suggestions on how things may run smoother or better. As you know from an earlier chapter, this is an important principle in basic philosophy of Kaizen.

12 ways that you can help to improve initiative at work:

1. **Ask what-if** - Make a habit of asking "what if" type of questions instead of simply accepting the status-quo. Everyone on the organization chart should be encouraged to look at everyday situations and ask "what-if" type questions.
2. **Brainstorm** - Schedule creative brainstorming sessions with your teams, or as an individual try and brainstorm on your own. This simply means giving people the opportunity to consider and express virtually any idea without the fear of ridicule. The hope is that if enough

smart and talented people throw enough suggestions against the wall that it will ultimately pay huge dividends for an organization.

3. **Find a mentor** – Finding a mentor can give you a valuable resource within an organization (or perhaps from outside the company) that can help validate your ideas before you push them up the ladder. Often times these people can give you a better lay of the land and help you steer through some of the politics and or historical issues that exists within most organizations, especially if you are new to the group.

4. **Be vocal** – The next time someone asks you for your opinion don't be afraid to express your thoughts. You'll need to be respectful so as not to alienate yourself, but there is nothing wrong with sharing your ideas and thoughts with the rest of your team.

5. **Be active** - If you see something that needs to be done, or if you see a team mate that needs help, then just do it even if it is not a part of your responsibility. This is a key part of being a good team player, but your involvement in new things will also give you fresh insight into other areas within the organization and perhaps allow you to make recommendations on how things might be improved.

6. **New opportunities** - Take advantage of new opportunities that frequently present themselves in most organizations. Offer your services to help fix situations, implement new software packages, or create new marketing ideas. You will certainly garner some recognition and as your ideas flourish you will make name for yourself in the organization as a problem solver.

7. **Focus your efforts** – Don't try to fix everything at once. Review all of the situations around you and make a list of what areas can be improved. Pick one and brainstorm what you can do to make it better. Depending upon the situation you should discuss your

idea with your supervisor before you attempt to implement it on your own.

8. **No Fear** - If you want something, and you know that you are right then keep at it. You don't want to be a pest, but people and opinions change over time. Don't let the fear of failure or rejection hold you back.

9. **Ask for help** - We probably all have friends at home and at work with varying skills and backgrounds. Many times we run across people in our lives with a high level of expertise that may be outside of our experience. Approach these people and ask for their help. Most decent people will be glad to share their knowledge with you and it will be a good way for you to increase your expertise. Early on in my career I surrounded myself with people that had a strong background in IT. I constantly asked them how things worked and for them to explain the latest technology and terminology to me. The help I received from these people was extremely valuable to me, especially when desktop PC's were just taking hold in the business world.

10. **Volunteer** - Find informal leadership positions within or outside of your organization. Suggest that you start a fund raising campaign at work in order to give back to your community. Show your teammates and supervisor that you don't need to wait for someone else to tell you what to do and that you are a leader. As the program develops people will begin to notice your planning and organizing skills which will most certainly help in the continued development of your career.

11. **Be a problem solver** - Instead of running to your supervisor with the latest problem, stop and evaluate the situation. Try and find out how the problem can be solved BEFORE you address it with your boss. I guarantee that you will be recognized for these endeavors and that you will be one of the first people that your manager turns to when he or she needs help.

12. **An eye to the future** – Take a look around your organization and discuss the future with your mentor. Try to uncover something new that is scheduled to take place that you can prepare for in advance. When the new situation/idea/product is announced then you can step up and offer your assistance.

Famous examples of initiative

A very famous example of someone who displayed incredible initiative comes to us from James Dyson the creator of the now famous Dyson Vacuum Cleaner. Wikipedia posted information that I have summarized below that clearly illustrates this point:

> *In the late 1970s, Dyson had the idea of using cyclonic separation to create a vacuum cleaner that would not lose suction as it picked up dirt. He became frustrated with his Hoover Junior's diminishing performance as dust kept clogging the bag and reducing the suction. The bagless, cyclone idea came from the spray-finishing room's air filter in his Ballbarrow factory.*

> *Unfortunately, no manufacturer or distributor would handle his product in the UK, as it would disturb the valuable market for replacement dust bags. Given the circumstances Dyson launched it in Japan through catalogue sales as the "G-Force" cleaner in 1983. Manufactured in bright pink, the G-Force sold for the equivalent of £2,000 and it won the 1991 International Design Fair prize in Japan. He obtained his first U.S. patent on the idea in 1986 (U.S. Patent 4,593,429).*

> *Dyson's breakthrough in the UK market came more than ten years after his initial idea. It occurred through a TV advertising campaign in which it was emphasized that unlike most of its rivals, his new device did not require the continuing purchase of replacement bags.*

At that time, the UK market for disposable cleaner bags was £100 million. The slogan "say goodbye to the bag" proved more attractive to the buying public than a previous emphasis on the suction efficiency that its technology delivers. Ironically, the previous step change in domestic vacuum cleaner design had been the introduction of the disposable bag in which users were willing to pay extra for the convenience. The Dyson Dual Cyclone became the fastest-selling vacuum cleaner ever made in the UK, which outsold those of some of the companies that rejected his idea and has become one of the most popular brands in the UK.

I find it very interesting that the vacuum began to sell so well because of the fact that the new vacuum had no bag and not because of Mr. Dyson's original focus on eliminating a lack of suction. This should give many marketing departments a lot of food for thought when trying to create promotional campaigns for their new products.

Regardless of why it was so popular, the fact that Dyson took the initiative to create his unique and now ubiquitous, cyclonic vacuum should be a beacon of light for anyone who has ever been nervous or skeptical about trying to do things in a new way.

Another extremely famous example of initiative comes to us businessideaslab.com when they published this information about UPS:

__United Parcel Service, or UPS__ as it is known by everyone today, is one of the largest messenger and courier services on the planet. Working out of the shipment and logistics industry, the company has left its mark on the world, and for over a century, it has provided cost effective and reliable messenger services not just in America, but all over the world. It provides parcel delivery services in over 200 countries and *operates its own carrier goods, airline services to ensure the very best services to its clients.*

The company has grown to become a giant and delivers well over 15 million packages globally on a daily basis, but when it first started out over a hundred years ago, no one could have predicted UPS would be such a roaring success.

James Casey founded UPS back in 1907 with the initial name of American Messenger Company. He was only 19 years old and had to ask a friend for a loan of $100 to start the company, which was registered in Seattle, Washington. His first business was mainly delivering messages and small packages from people to other people. The young entrepreneur had worked as a messenger for several similar services in the city. The need for reliable messenger service existed in the market, and Casey capitalized on this need, with tremendous results.

His principle had been always to deliver the best services for low prices, and the modern day UPS still holds true to that promise. His own brother and a few friends worked as delivery boys and delivered most of the goods on foot, or used bikes for the more distant destinations. There were almost no automobiles in those times.

A small office rented out in the basement served as the first base for UPS, and through Casey's firm stance on quality, the company was able to beat the competition from existing companies and emerged as the city's favorite messenger service.

After 1913, a device invented by a guy named Alexander Bell – the telephone – had begun getting more and more popular among people. This decreased the demand for messaging services and American Messenger Company had to reorganize its activities. They focused more on package deliveries and bought some motorcycles for improving their services. This was also the time that the company acquired one of its first cars for delivering heavier goods, a Model T Ford. Casey and his new partner Claude Ryan partnered up with a competitor Evert McCabe and changed the name of the newly formed company to Merchants Parcel Delivery, a name which the company continued using till 1937, when the name was officially changed to the modern day United Parcel Service.

By 1918 a few big department stores in Seattle were attracted as customers. The stores had their own delivery cars, but turned excess business over to Merchants Parcel Delivery. After 1919 the company started offering services in Oakland as well.

Services were expanded to other major cities in the country, including New York, and soon UPS was offering its services in all 48 contiguous states in the US. It was around this time that consolidated delivery services were first introduced, and UPS was one of the pioneers of this technique. All shipments to a neighborhood were delivered by a single person using one delivery car, making it more cost effective for the company to operate over a large area. In 1988 UPS launched its own airline for enhanced delivery services and shifted its office once again to the present location in Sandy Springs, Georgia.

Acquisition of strategic services

UPS always pushed the curve and ensured that it had the best supply chain network by acquiring companies that could help UPS improve its delivery services. Haulfast and Carryfast, two well established supply chain solutions were bought by UPS in 1992, and turned into the official supply chain vendor for the company. The company did something similar to US and Blue Label Air back in 1982 in order to provide faster delivery service to its customers. Through acquisition or strategic partnerships, UPS ensured that it always had an edge, and used its key alliances to offer competitive services not just in America but Canada, and several other countries as well.

Modern Day UPS

UPS celebrated a hundred years of successful operation in June, 2009. Being one of the most influential logistic and supply chain organizations in the world, UPS continues to offer new services to its customers. The services of personal mailboxes were offered to clients in 2003 after UPS acquired Mail Boxes Etc. As of May, 2014, UPS has a market cap of $89.65 billion US dollars and a part of the 50 most valuable brands in the world. It continues to grow and has emerged as the first choice for anyone who requires reliable and cost effective parcel delivery services.

Henry Ford

In a previous chapter I discussed Henry Ford and some of the great ideas he implemented in his business. He once was asked about giving customers what they wanted and his reply was quite prophetic, and a clear sign that the man knew the importance of taking the initiative. His statement:

> *"If I had asked my customers, they would have told me that they wanted a faster horse!*

As a business owner or manager how often do you display this type of initiative? Perhaps not too often, as many people never reach the rarified heights as James Dyson, James Casey or Henry Ford. It is especially relevant when evaluating the path taken by UPS and how many times they have had to re-invent themselves over the years based upon new technology and trends in the market.

What you can do as a business owner or manager is to continue to evaluate your business situation and apply your initiative to strengthen your business. Look at all of the innovations that the Dyson brand continues to bring to the table such as new types of hand dryers and portable fans that are revolutionizing the market.

These companies continue to be successful because of the initiative displayed by the people heading up these organizations that allows for creative people and innovation to thrive. You can most certainly do this with your business, regardless of its size or history. It simply takes the drive and confidence to use your initiative, creativity and sound judgment for success.

Management checklist

- ✓ Do I demonstrate signs of initiative at work and encourage it to take place with my teammates?
- ✓ Do I reward acts of initiative within my teammates when the results turn out in a positive fashion?
- ✓ How do I handle acts of initiative when they do not turn out well? Do I discuss the situation with the person so that they can recognize a better way forward in the future, or do I get frustrated and angry with their efforts?
- ✓ Do I talk to my teammates about their own acts of initiative and the importance they will play in the future of our business?
- ✓ Can I clearly identify specific things that have been changed within my organization due to the initiatives taken by my team?

"The best way to not feel hopeless is to get up and do something. Don't wait for good things to happen to you. If you go out and make some good things happen, you will fill the world with hope, you will fill yourself with hope." — **Barack Obama**

"People who say it cannot be done should not interrupt those who are doing it." - **George Bernard Shaw**

"Be willing to make decisions. That's the most important quality in a good leader. Don't fall victim to what I call the ready-aim-aim-aim-aim syndrome. You must be willing to fire." - **T. Boone Pickens**

Chapter 15 – Vision

Creating a long term vision for your organization is an important responsibility for any business owner or manager. If it is done correctly it can be the glue that holds an organization together because it gives a clear focus to every effort and every activity of the business.

In order to create a long term, corporate vision you need to focus on two different, yet closely related topics:

1. The core characteristics of how you want your business to run on a daily basis that rarely change. Many of these are the items in The Pyramid of Business Success.
2. A long term view of what the company can and will look like in the future.

Before I go any further, it's important to note that it will be much easier to achieve the second item if you have the first one solidly in place. As you hopefully now recognize, this is actually one of the key points of this entire book.

Core characteristics

As a business owner or manager how you operate and interact with people on a day to day basis is one of the single biggest keys in creating a strong, vibrant and successful business. It sets the stage for your involvement with everyone that has a stake in your organization; from employees, to customers, to investors.

If you truly believe in the concepts of this book then you must make them part of your daily habits and in how you deal with things and people daily. They must become part of the vision that you create for your employees and customers. You may choose to create flyers or posters that affirm your belief in acting with integrity, hard work, enthusiasm, the importance of resilience and personal accountability. You may also want to discuss these attributes and characteristics with potential new employees and undergo steps to ensure that people you bring into your organization will be a good match. It's also crucial that everyone on your management team shares these characteristics and that they lead their teams through the utilization of these principles.

This type of vision needs to be much more than words on a piece of paper. But this is not always the case. I have seen many organizations that claim they truly value their employees yet they continually treat them poorly and without much respect. I have seen others that claim that they are interested in customer service, but make little, if any, effort to ensure that their customers are happy after the sale has taken place.

This type of vision without action is actually more harmful to an organization than no vision at all. The hypocrisy that your employees and customers witness will no doubt become a sore point and a source of ridicule that will erode your employees desire to work hard, be enthusiastic and to act with integrity. It will also ultimately cause your customers to take their business elsewhere.

A long term view

James Collins and Jerry Porras referred to this long term view as an "envisioned future" in an article published in the *Harvard Business Review Magazine.* Although written a number of years ago it still has a lot of value in today's business world. It is a little lengthy, but it is so important that I have provided an excerpt of some of the more salient points, which follows:

> *"We found in our research that visionary companies often use bold missions—or what we prefer to call BHAGs (pronounced BEE-hags and shorthand for Big, Hairy, Audacious Goals)—as a powerful way to stimulate*

progress. All companies have goals. But there is a difference between merely having a goal and becoming committed to a huge, daunting challenge—such as climbing Mount Everest. A true BHAG is clear and compelling, serves as a unifying focal point of effort, and acts as a catalyst for team spirit. It has a clear finish line, so the organization can know when it has achieved the goal; people like to shoot for finish lines. A BHAG engages people—it reaches out and grabs them. It is tangible, energizing, highly focused. People get it right away; it takes little or no explanation. For example, NASA's 1960s moon mission didn't need a committee of wordsmiths to spend endless hours turning the goal into a verbose, impossible-to-remember mission statement. The goal itself was so easy to grasp—so compelling in its own right—that it could be said 100 different ways yet be easily understood by everyone. Most corporate statements we've seen do little to spur forward movement because they do not contain the powerful mechanism of a BHAG.

Although organizations may have many BHAGs at different levels operating at the same time, vision requires a special type of BHAG—a vision-level BHAG that applies to the entire organization and requires 10 to 30 years of effort to complete. Setting the BHAG that far into the future requires thinking beyond the current capabilities of the organization and the current environment. Indeed, inventing such a goal forces an executive team to be visionary, rather than just strategic or tactical. A BHAG should not be a sure bet—it will have perhaps only a 50% to 70% probability of success—but the organization must believe that it can reach the goal anyway.

…In addition to vision-level BHAGs, an envisioned future needs what we call vivid description—that is, a vibrant,

engaging, and specific description of what it will be like to achieve the BHAG. Think of it as translating the vision from words into pictures, of creating an image that people can carry around in their heads. It is a question of painting a picture with your words. Picture painting is essential for making the 10-to-30-year BHAG tangible in people's minds.

For example, Henry Ford brought to life the goal of democratizing the automobile with this vivid description: "I will build a motor car for the great multitude... It will be so low in price that no man making a good salary will be unable to own one and enjoy with his family the blessing of hours of pleasure in God's great open spaces... When I'm through, everybody will be able to afford one, and everyone will have one. The horse will have disappeared from our highways, the automobile will be taken for granted...[and we will] give a large number of men employment at good wages."

The components-support division of a computer-products company had a general manager who was able to describe vividly the goal of becoming one of the most sought-after divisions in the company: "We will be respected and admired by our peers... Our solutions will be actively sought by the end-product divisions, who will achieve significant product 'hits' in the marketplace largely because of our technical contribution... We will have pride in ourselves... The best up-and-coming people in the company will seek to work in our division... People will give unsolicited feedback that they love what they are doing... [Our own] people will walk on the balls of their feet... [They] will willingly work hard because they want to... Both employees and customers will feel that our division has contributed to their life in a positive way."

Passion, emotion, and conviction are essential parts of the vivid description. Some managers are uncomfortable expressing emotion about their dreams, but that's what motivates others. Churchill understood that when he described the BHAG facing Great Britain in 1940. He did not just say, "Beat Hitler." He said, "Hitler knows he will have to break us on this island or lose the war. If we can stand up to him, all Europe may be free, and the life of the world may move forward into broad, sunlit uplands. But if we fail, the whole world, including the United States, including all we have known and cared for, will sink into the abyss of a new Dark Age, made more sinister and perhaps more protracted by the lights of perverted science. Let us therefore brace ourselves to our duties and so bear ourselves that if the British Empire and its Commonwealth last for a thousand years, men will still say, 'This was their finest hour.'"

...It makes no sense to analyze whether an envisioned future is the right one. With a creation—and the task is creation of a future, not prediction—there can be no right answer. Did Beethoven create the right Ninth Symphony? Did Shakespeare create the right Hamlet? We can't answer these questions; they're nonsense. The envisioned future involves such essential questions as Does it get our juices flowing? Do we find it stimulating? Does it spur forward momentum? Does it get people going? The envisioned future should be so exciting in its own right that it would continue to keep the organization motivated even if the leaders who set the goal disappeared. City Bank, the predecessor of Citicorp, had the BHAG "to become the most powerful, the most serviceable, the most far-reaching world financial institution that has ever been"—a goal that generated excitement through multiple generations until it was achieved. Similarly, the NASA moon mission continued to galvanize people even though President John F.

Kennedy (the leader associated with setting the goal) died years before its completion.

To create an effective envisioned future requires a certain level of unreasonable confidence and commitment. Keep in mind that a BHAG is not just a goal; it is a Big, Hairy, Audacious Goal. It's not reasonable for a small regional bank to set the goal of becoming "the most powerful, the most serviceable, the most far-reaching world financial institution that has ever been," as City Bank did in 1915. It's not a tepid claim that "we will democratize the automobile," as Henry Ford said. It was almost laughable for Philip Morris—as the sixth-place player with 9% market share in the 1950s— to take on the goal of defeating Goliath RJ Reynolds Tobacco Company and becoming number one. Indeed, the envisioned future should produce a bit of the "gulp factor": when it dawns on people what it will take to achieve the goal, there should be an almost audible gulp.

But what about failure to realize the envisioned future? In our research, we found that the visionary companies displayed a remarkable ability to achieve even their most audacious goals. Ford did democratize the automobile; Citicorp did become the most far-reaching bank in the world, and Philip Morris did rise from sixth to first and beat RJ Reynolds worldwide.

In contrast, the comparison companies in our research frequently did not achieve their BHAGs, if they set them at all. The difference does not lie in setting easier goals: the visionary companies tended to have even more audacious ambitions. The difference does not lie in charismatic, visionary leadership: the visionary companies often achieved their BHAGs without such larger-than-life leaders at the helm. Nor does the

234

difference lie in better strategy: the visionary companies often realized their goals more by an organic process of "let's try a lot of stuff and keep what works" than by well-laid strategic plans. Rather, their success lies in building the strength of their organization as their primary way of creating the future.

Let's look at that last sentence again:

"… their success lies in building the strength of their organization as their primary way of creating the future."

This entire book is about trying to help business owners and managers build the strength of their organization. This is why it is so important to build your organization upon the characteristics at the very base of The Pyramid of Business Success. The research published years ago makes it clear that BHAGs can only be attained with a strong organization, built from the bottom up and through the successful applications of the characteristics in this book.

Things to consider

Creating an appropriate vision or BHAG may be easy for some owners and more difficult for others. If you typically struggle with this type of business matter then you should consider the following five items to help you build your corporate vision:

1. **Be inspirational and passionate when discussing your vision** - The way you present your vision is just as important as the content. Your confidence, tone of voice and enthusiasm will help to paint a lasting picture to everyone you meet and allow them to feel comfortable with where the company is headed. People must feel that you believe in what you are saying and want to go along for the ride!

2. **Even if it is not a true BHAG, make your vision challenging** – You may not have the desire to be the next Ford Motor Company or Citicorp, but your vision still needs to be a challenge to the people on your team. No one will get any value out of creating and reaching goals and visions that were too easy to attain.

3. **Make it clear and relatively simple** - Making your vision of the future easy to understand is critical. Years ago the vision of Disney was "to make people happy". Long, detailed corporate speak often becomes boring and meaningless to most people. Today, the Disney Mission/Vision statement is a blur of words.

> *"The mission of The Walt Disney Company is to be one of the world's leading producers and providers of entertainment and information. Using our portfolio of brands to differentiate our content, services and consumer products, we seek to develop the most creative, innovative and profitable entertainment experiences and related products in the world."*

4. **Relate it to their tasks** – Everyone in your organization needs to see how their day-to- day activities will help the organization reach their long term vision. This is very important as some people that perform what is often considered to be menial tasks often don't realize that they play a role in the success of an organization. Show everyone on your team how they help you achieve your vision and reward them with praise and recognition as often as possible.

5. **Make it inclusive and team oriented** – Always remember that you cannot attain your vision or BHAGs alone. You're not an island and the success

of your business rests on the strength of your people much more so than on your individual efforts. Be sure your vision includes terms such as "we", "us" and "our". Your team will help ensure success and you need to let them know that right from the start.

Visionary leadership is not necessarily relegated to the business world. Many fine examples can be found by examining social and historical leaders that played significant roles in shaping the 20th century. One of the best examples can be found by evaluating the actions of Martin Luther King and an excerpt from his famous *"I Have a Dream"* speech:

> *"...I say to you today, my friends, so even though we face the difficulties of today and tomorrow, I still have a dream. It is a dream deeply rooted in the American dream.*
>
> *I have a dream that one day this nation will rise up and live out the true meaning of its creed: "We hold these truths to be self-evident: that all men are created equal."*
>
> *I have a dream that one day on the red hills of Georgia the sons of former slaves and the sons of former slave owners will be able to sit down together at the table of brotherhood.*
>
> *I have a dream that one day even the state of Mississippi, a state sweltering with the heat of injustice, sweltering with the heat of oppression, will be transformed into an oasis of freedom and justice.*
>
> *I have a dream that my four little children will one day live in a nation where they will not be judged by the color of their skin but by the content of their character. I have a dream today.*

I have a dream that one day, down in Alabama, with its vicious racists, with its governor having his lips dripping with the words of interposition and nullification; one day right there in Alabama, little black boys and black girls will be able to join hands with little white boys and white girls as sisters and brothers.

I have a dream today."

Remarkable! The powerful image that his words created at that time still resonates today. He was a true force of nature that forever altered our government, society and culture. His vision was a little longer than I would recommend for any business, but it carried the hopes of an entire segment of our population.

We cannot all be as gifted an orator as Dr. King, but we can and should rely on his expertise in motivation to help us create our own vision. His words might help inspire a vision for your business success, or perhaps something even more important. It is up to you to create this vision and to build it upon sound characteristics that will resonate with your team members and customers.

Be confident, be bold, be a visionary and be successful!

Management Checklist

- ✓ Do I demonstrate the characteristics at the base of the Pyramid of Success each and every day?
- ✓ Do I expect that everyone on my team abides by the elements in The Pyramid of Business Success?
- ✓ Do I make it clear how the elements in The Pyramid of Business Success contribute to our corporate vision and the role everyone plays in attaining our goals?
- ✓ Have I set any BHAGs for our company that will push us to new heights?

- ✓ Have I clearly conveyed our corporate vision to everyone on my team and would they be able to tell me what it is if asked?

"Vision is the art of seeing what is invisible to others "- **Jonathan Swift**

"Good leaders must communicate vision clearly, creatively, and continually. However, the vision doesn't come alive until the leader models it." – **John C. Maxwell**

"Good business leaders create a vision, articulate the vision, passionately own the vision, and relentlessly drive it to completion" – **Jack Welch**

Chapter 16 - Work-Life Balance

The website businessdictionary.com defines this topic in the following fashion:

> " A comfortable state of equilibrium achieved between an employee's primary priorities of their employment position and their private lifestyle. Most psychologists would agree that the demands of an employee's career should not overwhelm the individual's ability to enjoy a satisfying personal life outside of the business environment."

With the exception of the most hardened business leaders, most people would say that attaining a solid work-life balance is a good thing for most people. Yet in practice many people find this to be quite difficult to accomplish especially as they rise through the ranks of management. For years this key aspect of long term happiness has been overlooked throughout the US market and undeniably, many successful businesses have been created without this taking place.

The workforce is changing, however, and if business owners and managers want to maintain their success they may want to consider changing some practices that will enable their employees to attain this state of equilibrium. Given the importance the influential "Millennials" will continue to play in our workforce, creating an environment that will allow this to happen will become increasingly important throughout the next few decades.

In case you are not aware, Lydia Abbot posted an article on LinkedIn about Millennials that contained the following statement:

"Millennials aren't as willing as former generations to sacrifice their personal life in order to advance their careers. They like to "work hard – play hard" and want to be at a company that appreciates this desire for balance. They also expect a more flexible work environment than previous generations and want to work for a company that supports various causes."

Every article that I found identified the strong desire on the part of "Millenials" or "Generation-Y" for a solid work-life balance. A business owner or manager will be making a mistake by not recognizing this and taking it into consideration as he/she lays the groundwork for how they operate their organization.

Current situation

20somethingfinance.com published the following data that clearly illustrates my previous point that many of us are currently suffering from the lack of a true work-life balance. A lot of this is due to the amount of hours we work and the lack of free time we actually receive, especially if we compare ourselves to the rest of the industrialized world:

American Average Work Hours:

- *At least 134 countries have laws setting the maximum length of the work week; the U.S. does not.*
- *In the U.S., 85.8 percent of males and 66.5 percent of females work more than 40 hours per week.*
- *According to the International Labor Organization, "Americans work 137 more hours per year than Japanese workers, 260 more hours per year than British workers, and 499 more hours per year than French workers."*
- *Using data by the U.S. Bureau of Labor Statistics, the average productivity per American worker has increased 400% since 1950. One way to look at that is that it should only take one-quarter of the work hours, or 11*

hours per week, to afford the same standard of living as a worker in 1950 (or our standard of living should be 4 times higher). Is that the case? Obviously not. Someone is profiting, it's just not the average American worker.

American Paid Vacation Time & Sick Time:

- *There is not a federal law requiring paid sick days in the United States.*
- *The U.S. remains the only industrialized country in the world that has no legally mandated annual leave.*
- *In every country except Canada and Japan (and the U.S., which averages 13 days/per year), workers get at least 20 paid vacation days. In France and Finland, they get 30 – an entire month and a half off, paid, every year*

A number of other studies have been completed that clearly illustrate that Americans actually suffer from a work-life *imbalance!* Mother Jones published data indicating that most people, especially those listed as professional or middle income men and women are working many more hours than in the past.

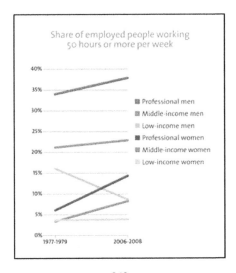

Mother Jones also published the graphics below to illustrate how US companies compare to the rest of the world on paid annual leave.

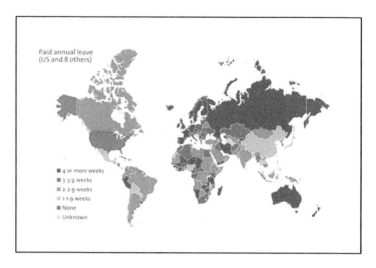

In case the graphics are difficult to see, US companies are not required to offer any paid annual leave

... or paid maternity leave.

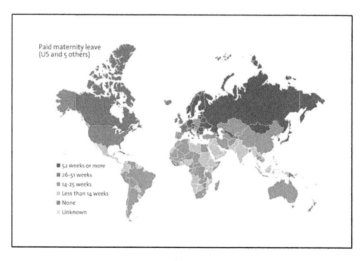

Also from Mother Jones:

As illustrated by a survey of employed email users, Americans are also expected to work outside of normal business hours.

	Digital Overtime
22%	are expected to respond to work email when they're not at work
50%	check work email on the weekends
46%	check work email on sick days.
34%	check work email while on vacation

You might think that with the extra hours worked and the ever increasing productivity gains that American workers would be earning a lot more as well. For the most part, however, wages have actually stagnated for most Americans as illustrated from the graph below:

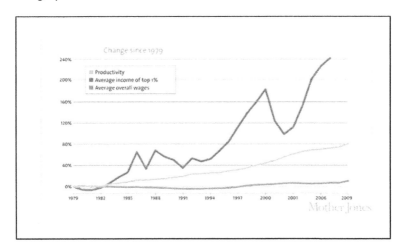

It is interesting to note that if the median household income had kept pace with the economy since 1970, it would now be nearly $92,000, not $50,000.

ABC News reported the following in 2008:

"Recent studies have painted a grim picture of the American working world: Longer days, less vacation time, and later retirement, and — and that was all during the good years of the 1990s.

The last few months have done nothing to ease those conditions, adding job insecurity to the mix as an increasing number of companies lay off workers to "downsize" in the slumping economy.
Those lucky enough to still have a job can expect to be asked to do more, to make up for the "streamlined" workforce.

If organizations truly cared about their employees they would figure out a way to fix these situations. Many people argue that this situation does not need to be fixed and that it is this very work ethic that separates the US from everyone else in the world. Perhaps they are right, but it's clear that other *"westernized"* countries have adopted more flexible work environments and still remain extremely competitive.

I can just hear the words being muttered right now…socialist…communist…if you don't like it here then go live in Europe. It is amazing to me that American workers have allowed themselves to be brainwashed in such a fashion. The report from ABC continues:

Not only are Americans working longer hours than at any time since statistics have been kept, but now they are also working longer than anyone else in the industrialized world. And while workers in other countries have been seeing their hours cut back by legislation focused on preventing work from infringing on private life, Americans have been going in the other direction.

*A trio of recent books, **The White-Collar Sweatshop** by Jill Andresky Fraser, **The Overworked American** by Juliet Schor, and **The Working Life** by Joanne B. Ciulla, have been embraced by a public that apparently feels harassed by the pressures of the workplace.*

Road rage, workplace shootings, the rising number of children placed in day care and the increasing demand on schools to provide after-school activities to occupy children whose parents are too busy have all been pointed to as evidence that Americans are overstressed and overworked.

Bureau of Labor statistics released last year confirmed what Fraser had been hearing in four years of interviews with white-collar workers. In 1999, more than 25 million Americans - 20.5 percent of the total workforce - reported that they worked at least 49 hours a week, and 11 million of those said they worked more than 59 hours a week. "

Despite my own strong, ingrained work ethic, I view this lack of emphasis on work-life balance as powerful organizations not caring enough about their workers, all in the name of profits. Again, I ask the people responsible for creating this environment to explain how other countries can remain competitive and profitable and still provide their workers with a better balance between their work life and their private life.

In one of the most blatant examples of blaming the victim, here's an article written by Dr. Tomas Chamorro-Premuzic, and published by the *Harvard Business Review*:

…"Overworking is really only possible if you are not having fun at work. By the same token, any amount

247

of work will be dull if you are not engaged, or if you find your work unfulfilling.

Maybe it's time to redefine the work-life balance — or at least stop thinking about it. Here are some considerations:

Hard work may be your most important career weapon. *Indeed, once you are smart-enough or qualified to do a job, only hard work will distinguish you from everyone else. Workaholics tend to have higher social status in every society, including laidback cultures like those found in the Caribbean, Mediterranean, or South America. Every significant achievement in civilization (from art to science to sport) is the result of people who worked a lot harder than everyone else, and also happened to be utterly unconcerned about maintaining work-life balance. Exceptional achievers live longer, and they pretty much work until their death. Unsurprisingly, the 10 most workaholic nations in the world account for most of the world's GDP.*

Engagement is the difference between the bright and the dark side of workaholism. *Put simply, a little bit of meaningless work is a lot worse for you than a great deal of meaningful work. Work is just like a relationship: Spending one week on a job you hate is as dreadful as spending a week with a person you don't like. But when you find the right job, or the right person, no amount of time is enough. Do what you love and you will love what you do, which will also make you love working harder and longer. And if you don't love what you are doing right now, you should try something else — it is never too late for a career change.*

Technology has not ruined your work-life balance; it has simply exposed how boring your work and your life used to be. Did you ever try to figure out why it is so hard to stop checking your smartphone, even when you are having dinner with a friend you haven't seen in ages, celebrating your anniversary, watching a movie, or out on a first date? It's really quite simple: None of those things are as interesting as the constant hum of your e-mail, Facebook, or Twitter account. Reality is over-rated, especially compared to cyberspace. Technology has not only eliminated the boundaries between work and life, but also improved both areas.

People who have jobs, rather than careers, worry about work-life balance because they are unable to have fun at work. If you are lucky enough to have a career — as opposed to a job — then you should embrace the work-life imbalance. A career provides a higher sense of purpose; a job provides an income. A job pays for what you do; a career pays for what you love. If you are always counting the number of hours you work (e.g., in a day, week, or month) you probably have a job rather than a career. Conversely, the more elusive the boundaries between your work and life, the more successful you probably are in both. A true career isn't a 9-5 endeavor. If you are having fun working, you will almost certainly keep working. Your career success depends on eliminating the division between work and play. Who cares about work-life balance when you can have work-life fusion?

Complaining about your poor work-life balance is a self-indulgent act. The belief that our ultimate aim in life is to feel good makes no evolutionary *sense. It stems from a distorted interpretation of positive psychology, which, in fact, foments self-improvement and growth rather than narcissistic self-indulgence. This misinterpretation explains why so many people in the industrialized Western world seek attention by complaining about their poor work-life balance. It may also explain the recent rise of the East vis-à-vis the West — you will not see many people in Japan, China, or Singapore complain about their poor work-life, even though they often work a lot harder. Unemployment and stagnation are in part the result of prioritizing leisure and pleasure over work.*

In short, the problem is not your inability to switch off, but to switch on. This is rooted in the fact that too few people work in careers they enjoy. The only way to be truly successful is to follow your passions, find your mission, and learn how to embrace the work-life imbalance."

Wow. After reading this I was almost speechless. The author places the blame for any negative effects of work-life imbalance squarely upon the shoulders of the worker. It is **your fault** poor worker that you suffer. You have chosen a bad job and that is why you are unhappy. If you had a better job you would not feel like you have an imbalance. And the pièce de résistance...you should not expect to feel good because it makes no evolutionary sense.

Amazing. I doubt that the robber barons of the late 1800's could have said it any better.

What can be done?

Fixing this situation is not something that will likely get resolved anytime soon. Most large, powerful (and myopic) organizations are not all of a sudden going to provide pay raises, cut back on the amount of work they expect from their workers, and provide more free time to their employees. There is often too much *perceived* pressure from the stock market for a lot of publicly traded organizations to react much differently.

As an individual it is important for you to keep an eye on the situation before you experience the negative effects of a work life imbalance. The website undercoverrecruiter.com published this "quiz" on work life balance that you may want to review:

- *Are you taking your work home with you, perhaps you even work while on the train or bus to work?*
- *Do you work more than 40 hours per week?*
- *Do your colleagues contact you out of hours or when you are on leave?*
- *Do you find yourself reading/replying to work emails over the weekend on your smart phone?*
- *Is it difficult for you to take time off to attend events such as your child's birthday or school sports day?*
- *Are you exhausted when you get home, keeping you from fulfilling your family commitments?*
- *Do you spend enough time with your family? Are the kids always in bed when you get home?*
- *Do you find you have no time to spend on self-development, or your favorite hobby?*
- *Do you lie in bed at night thinking about work issues?*
- *Are you stressed about your work?*

If you answered "yes" to many of these questions then you probably have a problem with work-life balance.

Blogger Annabel Candy posted the following advice that is also certainly worth considering:

"If you're feeling dissatisfied, stressed out, depressed, over-worked, unloved or worn out then there could be one of several things missing in your life. When you have a look through the list below you'll probably know which areas are being neglected and which areas are bogging you down. Working out what's lacking in your life is the key to restoring the balance and getting back your mojo."

How to Retune Your Work-Life Balance

1. Shift your priorities.

- *Decide what's lacking in your life, which areas need to be focused on to create more balance and make time for them.*
- *It is nice to believe your employer, business, family or friends would fall apart without you. It's flattering to consider yourself an indispensable part of the economy and people's lives. But sadly it's not true. It's a chimera, a mirage which has seduced you into wandering off into the desert and probably left you feeling very thirsty too.*
- *Work out what your priorities lie and then make sure they really do come first.*

2. Seek winning combinations.

- *Wherever possible try to find activities that satisfy two or more areas of your needs at the same time. Try to create a balance by working from home or doing a job which you love and which is in line with your values.*
- *For example, going for a walk on the beach satisfies both my emotional and physical needs.*

If I walk with my husband it takes care of our relationship too. Working from home allows me to be there when my kids come home from school and hang out with them fulltime during the school vacation. Choosing web design and writing for my career satisfies my creative urges, indulges my desire to help other people and brings home the bacon.

3. Balance yourself first.

- *Be careful not to subjugate your needs to those of other people.*
- *A lot of us are people-pleasers who want to make other people happy. You can only be responsible for your own happiness and you owe it to the people you care about, the family and friends who also care about you to look out for yourself.*

4. Be present.

- *Keep work where it belongs and family in their place.*
- *Allow yourself the time to fully participate in each activity without worrying about what you have to do next or hurrying to move on to the next thing.*
- *Being passionate about something is good but you also need to create a balance and be able to engage fully in other activities.*
- *Balance is about not being one-dimensional but allowing you to get in touch with the multi-faceted parts of your personality and unite them in a way that makes you feel happy.*
- *Remember life is more important than work. Life isn't something you fit in once your jobs have*

*been done. Life is your reason for being, not a
perk that comes from working.*

- *Yes, life is about creating balance and today is
  the time to start balancing your various needs. If
  you're not convinced you need to sort out your
  balance right now try turning Einstein's quote
  around like this: "Time's always moving on so
  we need to find balance or life will pass us by."*

The website undercoverrecruiter.com provides some
suggestions that a manager/owner might want consider as
well:

- *Allow your employees to work the hours they are
  employed to do, over 5 days and no more.*
- *Don't expect your team to work when they get home,
  unless you are offering a flexible working
  arrangement.*
- *Embrace flexible working arrangements, set clear
  expectations around these and give your team the
  chance to prove themselves working away from the
  office.*
- *Take a look at your parental leave policies, do they
  allow enough family time.*
- *Embrace cultural change and your employees
  differing commitments or beliefs.*
- *Allow your employees time during the workday to
  take a break (not just eat their lunch), encourage
  them to do something they enjoy like exercise or
  shopping or study.*
- *Reward your staff for high performance with extra
  time off work; add it to their annual leave balance to
  take when they wish.*
- *Do something special once in a while that they will
  remember, like take them out for the day to an
  event, or a team building exercise, or maybe just
  send everyone home at lunchtime on a Friday!*

It is too easy to forget that a happy employee is a productive employee. A major contributor to creating a happy employee is when they genuinely feel that they have a balance between their work and lifestyle commitments.

Just imagine how productive your team would be if they were all happy employees?

On a larger scale Stewart Friedman published an article for *Harvard Business Review* that proposed seven policy changes that need to be made so that parents can have kids and work at the same time. Although obviously written for a different purpose, many of his suggestions also apply to establishing a better work life balance.

1. ***Provide World-Class Child Care*** *- Our 2012 respondents were attuned to the fact that children require a caring person tending to their developmental needs. This was true for men as well as women. If Millennials want children – and realize wisely that children need to be cared for and that often both parents work outside the home – then we need to step up, as other countries have done, and invest in nurturing our young.*

2. ***Make Family Leave Universally Available*** *- Family leave, including paternity leave, is essential for giving parents the support they need to care for their children. Right now, according to the Bureau of Labor Statistics only 11 percent of U.S. employees receive paid family leave from employers. The one public policy that covers time off to care for new children, the Family and Medical Leave Act, laudable though it is, still excludes 40 percent of the workforce. And millions who are eligible and need leave don't take it, mainly because it's unpaid, but also*

because of the stigma and real-world negative consequences.

3. **Revise the Education Calendar** - *Revising the school calendar would be a benefit to children, to working parents, and to organizations that would, in the long run, have a better prepared workforce. Having children in school longer hours and for a greater part of the year is yet another way we as a society can help support young dual-career families so that they can envision a way of having their family and work lives in harmony rather than in perpetual discord*

4. **Support Portable Health Care** - *The Affordable Care Act is a step in this direction. It helps families obtain care while avoiding crippling debt as both parents might now have to navigate careers in which they move from job to job. And preventive care reduces the need for time off due to health problems that afflict workers and their children.*

5. **Display a Variety of Role Models and Career Paths** - *The more that young people hear stories about the wide range of noble, and economically viable, roles they can play in society, the easier it will be for them to choose the roles that match their talents and interests. Young adults would benefit from exploring as wide an array of career alternatives as possible, including and especially those that allow them to have the kind of autonomy and flexibility required to be engaged in both their careers and in their roles as parents.*

6. **Require Public Service** - *Young people are yearning to do work that benefits others. Our society could channel that enthusiasm and idealism by requiring a year of public service for postsecondary school youth, which would not only improve our workforce but would help all of us recalibrate what's really important. And it might help those young women who, as we observed, now*

*foresee a tradeoff between social impact via one's
career and motherhood, to envision instead a life in
which they can serve both the family of humanity and a
family with children of their own in the scope of their
lifetimes*

As I created this section I became frustrated at the lack of interest on the part of many businesses to fix this situation. Despite the recent recession, businesses in the US have become wealthy beyond belief. According to estimates made by Moody's Investors Services, the coffers of our largest organizations now hold over $1.5 trillion dollars. These organizations should take some of this money and help to improve the plight of the working person.

I am not talking about handouts, but raising the hourly pay rate for the middle class would be a start. It worked for Henry Ford at the early part of the 20th century; and despite what many conservative pundits might state, it will work in today's environment as well. Additionally, new workers could easily be added to help alleviate some of the existing stress placed on our existing and highly productive workforce. This would also enable organizations to provide additional paid time off to their loyal employees that would put us more in line with the rest of the industrialized world.

But many US business owners abhor these types of programs. They certainly work in other countries. Is it because the ideas are coming from foreign countries some of which have strong social programs?

As an ever evolving society we must be able to admit that we do not own all of the smart business or social ideas in the world. Other countries are experiencing success and we can learn from many of them if we just had the will to change. If you're an individual business owner you have the ability to help your employee's attain a solid work-life balance. It may mean re-thinking some closely held business beliefs, but other organizations are already proving that it can be done while still maintaining a solid level of profitability.

Jacquelyn Smith from *Forbes Magazine* published an article detailing a number of well known, profitable companies that are focused on helping their employees attain a strong work-life balance. A few examples follow:

> *The job search engine Indeed.com identified 25 of the biggest and brightest corporations that are going the extra mile to help employees achieve the elusive "work-life balance."*

> *To be considered for the list, each company had to have a minimum of 100 reviews on Indeed.com, and at least 1,000 employees (though most have a workforce that exceeds 10,000). This list excludes franchises, staffing firms, and government companies—but it does include international firms with over 100 jobs in the United States*

> ***Colgate-Palmolive*** *– Sits at top of Indeed's list of the 25 best big companies for work-life balance. Founded in 1806, the New York-based consumer products giant currently employs over 35,000 workers.*

> *"Work-life balance is often dependent on efficiency and professionalism; when management and employees are dedicated to their jobs and work hard during business hours, it gives them the flexibility to maintain a healthy personal life," Mike Steinerd the Director of Recruiting at Indeed.com says. "Past and present employees comment on the Colgate-Palmolive employer review page noting that management sets realistic expectations for employees, promotes time management skills and clearly communicates. In addition, Colgate-Palmolive offers some great benefits, such as flexible work hours,*

telecommute options, and nearby back-up childcare centers, which is a nice perk for work-at-home parents. As a result, Colgate-Palmolive has a high rate of employee retention, which is a testament to their culture."

Another company situated in the top three is **Coldwell Banker**, one of the oldest residential real estate franchise systems in North America. Founded in San Francisco in 1906, the New Jersey-based company currently employs 82,000 agents worldwide.

"Real estate is a unique industry because employees often have the freedom to create their own hours, and Coldwell Banker is no exception," Steinerd says. "Employees have characterized the company environment as having a 'work-hard-play-hard' type of attitude. For those people who are self-starters and independent workers, this is a great company."

Steinerd goes on to say that many of the companies on the list provide flexible work schedules and focus on teamwork. "Overall, the work environments tend to be friendly and the employees are determined to succeed, and there is the right balance of quality and quantity of work to be fulfilling."

For example, Walt Disney is recognized for their focus on training and team building, as well as the happiness of their employees, Steinerd says. And Google is known for "promoting flexible schedules and personal and professional balance, where employees learn how to manage their time, multitask and collaborate."

"We're seeing more and more that work-life balance is playing a key role in how employers are attracting top-talent," he adds. "Salary isn't the only factor a potential *employee is going to consider when they receive a job offer; they are often doing research on the company culture, looking at employer reviews and chatting with past or current employees. This is a growing trend we are noticing, so it's important that employers create workplaces that foster work-life balance. This list showcases those companies that according to previous or current employees got it right."*

Hopefully, this rings a bell as it relates to the information I cited pertaining to "Millenials" and the impact they are having on today's business world.

Still need more convincing?

Jessica Rohman a senior contributor at A Great Place To Work published an article entitled *"How Great Workplaces Support Work-Life Balance"* that further illustrates this point:

"...within the 100 Best Companies to Work For, an average of 83% of employees also believe they are encouraged to balance their work life and their personal life, and a whopping 91% of employees believe management allows them to take time off from work when they need to.

These numbers are impressive, and demonstrate that even in the face of zero paid vacation or holiday hours required for employees in the U.S., some organizations are taking it upon themselves to ensure employees have meaningful time off from work. Through their policies and practices, these organizations support employees as they strive to achieve a healthy balance between work life and personal life.

The information below illustrates the time off provided at the 100 Best Companies to Work For:

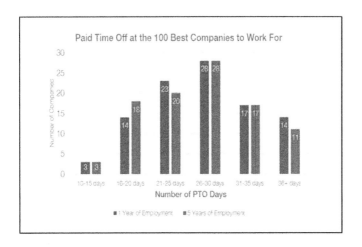

Paid Time Off at the 100 Best Companies to Work For

Additionally, with recent decades seeing a drastic increase in dual breadwinner roles in families, and in single-parent households, it is more important than ever for employees who are caregivers to have the ability to manage their family commitments in conjunction with their professional lives. With the rise of Millennials in the workforce, expectations regarding work/life balance are changing. According to the latest Price Waterhouse Coopers Next Gen Study, the majority of Millennials value balance to such an extent that they are "unwilling to commit to making work lives an exclusive priority, even with the promise of substantial compensation later on."

Workplaces that opt to care for their employees as people who have lives outside of work are providing solutions that help people manage both worlds, with ample opportunities for time off and flexible scheduling.

Consider these statistics. Of the 2014 FORTUNE 100 Best Companies:

- *85% offer telecommuting options*
- *82% offer over 20 days PTO after one year of employment*
- *80% offer flexible schedules*
- *78% offer a compressed workweek*
- *72% offer sabbaticals*

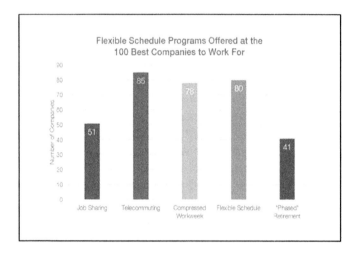

Some of the creative practices we've seen at this year's 100 Best Companies include the following examples:

At Darden Restaurants, based in Orlando, Florida, corporate employees have core hours from 9:00-3:30, but are given flexibility on arrival and departure times so they can manage their commutes and home obligations.

At Cisco, a Silicon-Valley based technology company, employees can opt for a "Ramp Up/Ramp Off" period to take 1-2 years off of work for a reason of their choosing.

Baptist Health South Florida created the "Centralized Staffing Center," where nurses with a minimum of two years of experience are invited to work at the facilities of their choosing while helping the organization fill short-staffed areas and maintaining patient quality and safety standards.

As expectations about work/life balance and modern family dynamics evolve, practices like these will become more normal as we look at the workplace of the future. And, as these options are more ubiquitous, they will increasingly become key factors for attracting top talent as they consider where, when, and how they would like to work.

Keep this chapter in mind when evaluating your corporate culture and business benefits. Would implementing better benefit programs simply be an additional expense or would they make your company more attractive to the very best workers? Would this type of investment help to strengthen the work-life balance for your employees and make them better workers on a daily basis? If we pay credence to any of the information in the preceding paragraphs then you would have to answer in the affirmative.

Helping your employees attain a solid work-life balance doesn't have to drive a business into bankruptcy. You can run a profitable business AND enable your employees to have a high quality of life outside of work. As a business owner/manager you owe it to yourself, your business and your employees to foster a positive work environment that will attract the very best talent and lead to long term business success.

Note: Some of the forms and graphs that are contained in this book may be a bit difficult to read since they were converted from color into black and white. For this reason, I have created a website that contains copies of each one for further review. The URL follows:

http://chrissopko.wix.com/pobs

"Work is a rubber ball. If you drop it, it will bounce back. The other four balls-- family, health, friends, integrity-- are made of glass. If you drop one of these, it will be irrevocably scuffed, nicked, perhaps even shattered." - **Gary Keller**

"You will never feel truly satisfied by work until you are satisfied by life." - **Heather Schuck**

"You will spend more of your waking hours at work than anything else. If that time doesn't make you happy it's a huge waste of life." - **Alexander Kjerulf**

Chapter 17 – Hiring the Right People

It's extremely important to uncover the best possible employees before you hire them. From the core principles of this book you want to ensure that your new people are bringing a high level of integrity, a desire to work hard, daily enthusiasm, an ability to be resilient, and personal accountability to your organization.

Here are some sample questions that you might want to use during your interview process to help identify the strengths and weaknesses of your candidates, especially as they relate to the each block of The Pyramid of Business Success.

Integrity and Honesty

1. Discuss a time when your integrity was challenged in your workplace. How did you handle the situation?
2. What would you do if you saw or heard an employee doing something dishonest?
3. In what business or work situation do you feel that honesty would be inappropriate? Please don't include things like commenting on an ugly dress or bad haircut.
4. What does integrity mean to you?
5. (FOR A SALES PERSON/MANAGER) What is more important to you, getting the sale or acting with honesty and integrity? Describe a time when you felt conflicted about this and let me know how you handled the situation.
6. (FOR A SALES MANAGER) How would you manage an extremely successful sales person that continually stretches the truth in order to close sales?
7. Do you speed while driving on the highway? (Most people do to some extent and it would be curious to have someone answer no.)
8. How do you earn the trust of others?
9. Describe a time in which you spoke up even though it might have been unpopular.

10. Describe a time when you admitted a mistake to your supervisor. What was the result and how did it make you feel?

Hard Work/Dedication

1. What is your definition of work ethic?
2. How did you pay for your college education?
3. At what age did you start working? What type of job was it? Did you work during high school?
4. Describe how you go above and beyond what is expected in your current role.
5. What was the last thing that you did outside of work that helped you develop your work related skills?
6. If I asked your last supervisor to tell me how often you showed up to work late what would he or she tell me? How do you feel about showing up to work late?
7. How do you feel about needing to stay after hours to complete a specific task?
8. Tell me about the job you have had in which you had to work the hardest? How did it make you feel?
9. If you had to rank yourself on a "competitive scale" from one to ten with one being the highest, where would you put yourself? Where would your last supervisor place you?
10. Describe one thing in your current role that you do not like to do. How do you motivate yourself to get it completed?

Enthusiasm

1. Describe a time in your current position in which you were truly motivated.
2. What parts of your job do you find boring and how do you overcome the situation?
3. Tell me about what you have been learning?
4. Tell me about your greatest business accomplishment.
5. Who is your role model and why?

6. Tell me about a time in which you needed to motivate others. How did you do it? What is the best way you've found to do this?
7. Describe a work environment where you work the best.
8. What role does your supervisor play in your daily motivation?
9. What motivates you?
10. A buzzword currently being used is "charisma". Tell me about your charisma and how you have utilized it in the past.

Resilience

1. What does the word resilience mean to you?
2. Describe a situation where you believed others were putting pressure on you. What did you do to manage this?
3. Have you ever "failed" at something? Describe the situation and what (if anything) did you learn?
4. As with many organizations, ours often includes multiple demands, shifting priorities, and sometimes short deadlines. In other words, sometimes the environment can be stressful. What do you do to keep on top of things and to refresh yourself when working in such an environment?
5. Tell me about a time when you had to adjust to someone's way of working to achieve a goal or complete a project?
6. Tell me about a time in which you decided to give up on a goal.
7. Tell me the details behind the last constructive criticism that you received from your supervisor and how you handled the situation.
8. You've been working very hard at work and your boss has finally seemed to take notice. You are actually in line for a promotion, but it is given to one of your colleagues. How would you react?
9. You are a sales person that has been working on an account for the last nine months and your main contact keeps telling you that the sale is yours. As you approach the decision day you get an email from the purchasing person that they have selected another vendor. What do you do?

10. When you think about the most difficult times you have faced in the past, what is your first thought? Are you angry, depressed, or simply glad that it is behind you?

Accountability

1. Describe a time in which you had to admit that you had made a mistake in your business career. What was the result?
2. Many people are often the victim of uncontrollable circumstances. Tell me how often this happens to you and describe how you typically react.
3. Describe what personal accountability means to you.
4. Tell me about a time in which you did not perform up to expectations. Why did this happen and what did you learn from the situation?
5. FOR A SALES PERSON/MANAGER – Why do you think that you typically lose a sale to a competitor? *(Unless you are selling commodities based upon price then be wary about anyone who gives you the answer of "price".)*
6. What would your immediate supervisor tell me is your biggest weakness? Would you agree with his/her assessment?
7. Tell me about a time that you failed to meet a commitment that you had made. What caused the situation to occur and what might you have done differently?
8. What, if anything, are you currently doing in order to improve from a professional standpoint?
9. Give me an example of someone you know whose personal actions led to disastrous results. How answerable is that person for what happened? What advice would you give to that person?
10. How do you deal with others who refuse to accept responsibility for issues in their area, but always blame something/someone else? What effect has this had on your or your team's work?

Goal Driven

1. Do you think that setting business goals is important for you? What about personal goals?
2. What goals, if any, did you set for yourself last year and did you achieve them?
3. Give me an example of a goal you were assigned that you did not achieve. Please tell me why you think this happened and what you learned from the experience?
4. Think about a job in which your goals were not clearly defined. How did you handle the situation and what did you learn?
5. Describe a time in which you set your sights too high.
6. Describe a time in which you set your sights too low.
7. What are your goals for the next 3-5 years?
8. What is the one thing that you would start working on today that will make a big difference in your life/career?
9. How do you keep track of your goals and your progress towards reaching them?
10. What is the most important goal you have ever set for yourself? Did you achieve it?

Customer Focused

1. How do you feel about the statement that the customer is always right?
2. Regardless of your company's policies, do you think it is right to provide a free maintenance call for a customer who owns a product that is one week out of warranty?
3. What are your thoughts about a sales person that adds on needless things to a quote in order to increase the overall value of the order he/she is planning on receiving?
4. Give me an example of when it is ok to lie to a customer.
5. How does it make you feel if you hear a colleague's phone ringing off the hook at work?
6. What does good customer service mean to you?

7. Describe a situation in which you were able to help turn around a dissatisfied customer into one that was very happy?
8. How do you think an organization should handle a situation in which an item that was previously promised for delivery to a customer is now back ordered?
9. Give me an example of a time you witnessed really great customer service.
10. What things can your current organization do in order to improve their customer service?

Team Builder

1. Describe how teamwork is exhibited in your current organization and what role do you play?
2. Do you prefer to work in a team environment or on your own? In which environment are you most effective?
3. Tell me about a time that you received help from someone else in your organization. How did it make you feel and what prompted the situation to occur?
4. How many times in a week/month do you need to help support your colleagues in getting their work done? How does this make you feel?
5. You are always able to complete your daily tasks, but some of your colleagues are not and you are constantly being asked to help bail them out. How does this make you feel? What would you do about the situation?
6. Describe a team based project in which you were a member. Were you able to achieve your goals? What role did you play and what were some of the difficulties you experienced?
7. What aspect of a typical team experience/project do you find frustrating?
8. How do you feel about team building activities at work? Are they successful or a waste of time?
9. FOR SALES PEOPLE – Have you ever worked in a team selling environment? How did it work and what caused frustration for you?

10. What would your current supervisor tell me about your desire to be a team player? What about your co-workers?

Communication

1. What steps do you take to ensure that confidential information does not make its way to the wrong people?
2. How would your supervisor rate your communication skills on a level of 1-10 with 10 being the best? What would they say you need to improve upon?
3. Do you think it is ever appropriate to lie to their supervisor or colleagues about a business situation? If yes, give me an example?
4. Do you feel that it is important for everyone in the business to know how well the organization is doing? Give your reasons for feeling this way.
5. Do you prefer email or face to face communication with your supervisor? Which do you feel is more effective
6. Your supervisor comes to you with a new project and provides you with an overview that lasts about 10-15 minutes of the things that she expects from you. After your meeting is over you realize that you are unclear about exactly what you are supposed to do. How do you handle the situation? Do you figure it out on your own? Do you ask a colleague for advice? Or something else?
7. Are you ever surprised to find out that people you work with misunderstood your meaning? How often does this happen and why do you think it happens?
8. What, if anything annoys you during communications with your colleagues?
9. FOR A MANAGER: Tell me about a time that you had to communicate delicate information to a person you supervised. How did you go about the process? Was it effective? What would you have done differently?
10. Tell me about a time that you had to communicate complex information to a colleague. How did you go about it and

what tools did you use? Was it effective? What would you have done differently?

Competitive

1. As a child, were you involved in sports? Was this an enjoyable experience? Why or why not?
2. Do you think that creating competition within work teams is good or bad? Please explain.
3. Tell me about a time that your competitive nature was at odds with working on a team? How did you handle the situation?
4. If I asked your supervisor how competitive you were on a scale of 1-10 with 10 being the highest, what would I be told? Would you agree and why?
5. At what point does competition within a team become a bad thing?
6. Describe a competitive situation in which you were involved? How long ago was it and how did it turn out?
7. Do you play games with your family or friends? Do the results of those games matter to you? How do you react when you lose?
8. Do you think there is a difference between being competitive at work and in games? Please explain.
9. Stories about the famous basketball player Michael Jordan belittling people on the court have been around for years. He was so competitive that he nearly destroyed the psyche of one of his teammates by continually calling him a loser. What are your thoughts when you hear about these types of situations?
10. In many sports geared towards children today no one gets cut from the team, everyone gets to play, and everyone gets a trophy at the end of the year even if they were not very good. What are your thoughts on this type of situation, and what if any role does this, or will this, play in today's business world?

Sound Judgment

1. What was the toughest decision you have had to make in the past five years? How did you make the decision, and how did it turn out?
2. What is more important when making an important decision, your gut feel or a solid evaluation of the situation?
3. Tell me about a time that you came to a different conclusion when evaluating an event or situation from your colleagues. Why do you think this occurred and who turned out to be correct?
4. Tell me about a time when you had to make a decision completely on your own. How did you make the decision and how did it turn out?
5. What is worse, making the wrong decision or no decision at all?
6. "New Coke" being released in 1985 was a disaster. Why do you think these types of situations happen even with a company like Coke that spends so much on market research?
7. FOR A MANAGER: You are a supervisor and two people in your department do not speak to each other. It is creating a tension in the group, but ALL of the daily work is being completed accurately and on a timely basis. Since the business side of things is going well would you do anything? If yes, what would you do?
8. You notice a major process in your department that is not working well. How do you handle the situation?
9. Tell me about the worst decision you have ever made at work. What, if anything would you do differently?
10. If I asked your supervisor to rank your judgment on a scale of 1-10 with 10 being the best what would I be told? Would you agree? Explain.

An Optimizer

1. What time management tools do you currently utilize? Please explain how you use them.
2. Describe your current working environment. What does it look like? Are you one of those neat-freaks that have everything extremely organized or is your desk a typical jumble of papers spread out everywhere? (This may seem so be a strangely worded question, but it is done deliberately in order to try and solicit a more frank response)
3. What specific steps have you taken in the past year to develop yourself, either at work or at home?
4. Do you feel that Kaizen type programs are effective or a waste of time?
5. What are the best ways in order to improve the performance of each department within your organization?
6. Have you undertaken any formal plans in the past that have significantly improved your organization from an operational aspect? Please provide details.
7. Have you ever been part of a team that was trying to make operational improvements at an organization that failed? Please describe the situation and what you learned?
8. What would be the first three things that you would do if you were given the opportunity to improve the operational aspects of a specific department within your current organization?
9. Do you feel that continuous improvement efforts are best developed and deployed from the top down?
10. What is the biggest challenge you face in your current role and what steps have you taken in the past year in order to fix the situation? Were you successful? If not, why?

Creativity

1. Tell me about the most creative thing you have ever done at work.
2. Tell me about the most creative thing you have seen someone else do at work.
3. Do you think that creativity is something that only certain people are born with?
4. Can creativity skills be developed?
5. How would you recommend that someone could discover their creative talent and cultivate it?
6. What was the best idea you contributed to your department over the past year?
7. How easy is it for you to try new things or new ways of doing something at work?
8. Can you give me an example of something that required a lot of creativity in which you were involved that did not turn out as planned? Why?
9. What would the title of your autobiography be?
10. What was the most recent type of problem that you have been called upon to try and fix? Why you?

Initiative

1. Tell me about a time that you undertook something on your own initiative in order to improve your individual performance.
2. Tell me about a time that you undertook a task on your own in order to improve a process or task at work.
3. Tell me about a time in which you identified a work related problem to your supervisor. How did you handle the situation? (look for someone that also offers a solution)
4. Are you the type of person that feels it is better to let your more experienced supervisor come up with a solution to a problem, or would you rather try and figure things out on your own?

5. You have been helping your supervisor prepare for a very important meeting that will take place next week. You have access to virtually all of the material, but the last piece of the puzzle is getting feedback from the rest of the team members. Your supervisor scheduled a staff meeting to discuss the situation, but is trapped at an out of town airport due to a snow storm. The staff meeting is scheduled for 2:00 today. What do you do?
6. You and your five colleagues have been assembled to discuss a new endeavor being considered by your company. You are presented with a number of known facts AND things that are still to be discovered. When asked for feedback on the situation, are you the first to answer? Why you and not someone else in the group?
7. When was the last time you volunteered for a new task within your current organization? What was it and how did it turn out?
8. What specific things did you do to prepare for this interview?
9. Your supervisor tells you and your entire team "just do as I tell you and nothing more." How does this make you feel?
10. We have all probably heard the old saying that there are "too many chiefs and not enough indians", or that there are "too many chefs in the kitchen". How do you feel about these statements and do you feel that you are a chief, chef, or a loyal employee that does what they are told?

Work-Life Balance

1. Many people talk about work-life balance. What does this mean to you? What specific steps have you undertaken in order to achieve it?
2. I had a friend that worked for a law firm and he continually worked 80 hour weeks. What are your thoughts on this type of situation?
3. How would you rank these four items in order of importance to you: Work, Family, Friends, and Supervisor?

4. Only 20% of people are satisfied with their work-life balance. Why do you think this is the case and what can be done to fix the situation?
5. Describe the general work-life balance at your last or current organization? Why do you think it was either good or bad?
6. What is the maximum number of hours that you feel a person should be willing to work on a continual basis each week?
7. Do you think that the quality of your work performance has anything to do with your personal life?
8. Many countries throughout the rest of the world require that employees give 5-6 weeks of vacation to their employees and up to six months of paid time off around the birth of a new baby. Do you think this is too much or are they on to something?
9. How would it make you feel if a team member was allowed to leave 15 minutes early each day in order to pick up their child and you were not because you did not have any children?
10. Has your spouse or significant other ever complained to you that you worked too much? How does this make you feel?

Obviously, you cannot, nor should you ask this complete list of over 150 interview questions when interviewing a potential candidate. Hopefully, it will give you some ideas, however, as to what you might ask given the specific areas that are most important to you and your organization.

Additional Information

In addition to asking the right types of questions I recommend that you always, always, always do a formal background check by a third-party service before you hire a person into your organization. This is an easy way to determine if someone has been disingenuous about their educational background, credentials, and any criminal record they may have. It's certainly better to uncover these items BEFORE someone is offered a position within your organization.

I also strongly recommend that you utilize a third-party testing service to evaluate skills and temperament for virtually any position within your organization. There are a number of companies in the market that can perform these tasks including one called Caliper that I have used successfully in the past. You need to find one that you feel comfortable with, but you will see that all of these organizations have studied the characteristics of successful people for many, many years and they have assembled a profile based upon the results from millions of people pertaining to what success looks like in different areas such as field sales, telesales, and customer service to name just a few. They will be happy to test your candidates on line and compare their results against their long history of data in order to determine whether or not the person is a good match to the successful profile they have assembled. You may have to spend a few hundred dollars per test, but it is well worth the investment.

In addition, have at least three people interview your final potential candidates before an offer is made. The interviews should be done separately with overlapping questions for each section that you find important. Afterwards, the team doing the interviewing can discuss each of the answers and compare notes. You will be surprised at what a fresh set of eyes and questions can uncover that might have been missed along the way. If the entire team does not feel that you have found the right person then move on and keep looking.

As you know from reading this book, hiring the right type of people that have a high level of integrity, who work hard, display enthusiasm on a day to day basis, are resilient, and accept accountability for their success are the keys to building a strong, long lasting and profitable business. Therefore it is crucial that you get it right the first time. Be thorough and trust your team to help you build a strong staff with attributes from the base of <u>The Pyramid of Business Success</u>.

Chapter 18 - Conclusion

I hope that this book has provided you with some insight into the personal characteristics and attributes that it takes to create and maintain a successful, long term business. Above and beyond the individual concepts I have provided you with some tools that you can use to further develop your skills as a manager, including sample interview questions that might help you uncover the best talent for your organization.

While none of the individual concepts or thoughts in this book is revolutionary, hopefully they will give you the impetus to really evaluate your business and how you currently operate. Maybe you had an "ah-ha" moment and recognized yourself or others in your organization when reading some of the examples, both good and bad. Perhaps you will undertake a new philosophy based upon these principles. As I mentioned in the introduction, if this book can help even one business become more successful then I will feel that the entire endeavor has been a success and certainly worthwhile.

The Pyramid of Business Success gets it strength form the core characteristics found in its lowest and most important level:

Base of the Pyramid – The Must Haves - The characteristics in the lowest level of my Pyramid are those that people either have or they don't when they enter your organization. Integrity, Hard Work, Enthusiasm, Resilience, and Personal Accountability are specific characteristics that MUST be present in you as a business owner or manager AND in any new person that joins your team. These are things that are typically ingrained into people during their earliest, developmental stages and you will be hard pressed to enhance these characteristics if they do not already have a strong foothold within you and at the very core of the people you hire.

It's very important for you to remember that none of the information contained in these pages will be beneficial unless they are actually *applied* on a daily basis. You need to assemble each of the building blocks contained in the entire Pyramid into a coherent, living package. Being goal driven, an optimizer, utilizing sound judgment, being competitive, and a team builder are all aspects that can be developed by virtually anyone with the willingness to learn. In order to help build a successful business these attributes must truly become part of your culture or else they are nothing more than empty words on a piece of paper.

Just like playing a musical instrument or learning a new sport the more you practice these skills and characteristics the better you will get. If you try to teach them to a person without a solid base then your experience will be like trying to swim through quicksand. In other words pretty darn difficult. If you start with the right core, however, and build the skills from the bottom up you will most certainly increase your likelihood of success.

The softer skills regarding creativity and initiative on the fourth level are where your true superstars will shine. Their ingenuity and insight will pay huge dividends to any organization looking for new solutions, especially if these people are given the ability to have continued influence within your organization.

Finally, EVERYTHING related to the business environment must be carefully tied into your vision of the future. You must be able to "paint" this vision so that it is easy to understand and so that people will want to get behind you and help you achieve it. This is why it is imperative that every other building block in The Pyramid of Business Success can be clearly related to making your vision become a reality.

Putting effort into the core of your company…your employees, will lead to success and ultimately admiration from your staff and peers. Each year *Fortune Magazine* publishes a list of the World's Most Admired Companies and for 2013 it follows:

1. Apple
2. Amazon
3. Google
4. Berkshire Hathaway
5. Starbucks

This is quite an exclusive list of names in which any business would be happy to have an affiliation, but let's look at each one and see how closely their values match up to elements of The Pyramid of Business Success.

1. **Apple** - Tim Cook's the CEO of Apple provided the following FTC memo that summarizes what he wants Apple to be about:

   "Apple is a company full of disruptive ideas and innovative people, who are also committed to upholding the highest moral, legal and ethical standards in everything we do. As I've said before, we believe technology can serve humankind's deepest values and highest aspirations. As Apple continues to grow, there will inevitably be scrutiny and criticism along our journey. We don't shy away from these kinds of questions, because we are confident in the integrity of our company and our coworkers."

2. **Amazon** - Jeff Bezos, the CEO of Amazon has identified a number of areas that he finds important to the long term success of his organization:

   - Obsess over the customer
   - We are willing to be misunderstood for long periods of time
   - Determine your customer's needs and work backwards
   - If you want to be inventive you have to be willing to fail

- Everyone has to be able to work in a call center
- This is day 1 for the Internet. We still have so much to learn

3. **Google** - The search engine and tech giant has a code of conduct posted on the webpage which I have summarized below:

- Serve our users
- Respect each other
- Avoid conflicts of interest
- Preserve confidentiality
- Protect Googles assets
- Ensure financial integrity and responsibility
- Obey the law

4. **Berkshire Hathaway** – Louis Kovacs posted five leadership lessons that we can all learn from Warren Buffet, founder of Berkshire Hathaway:

- **Lesson #1** - Hire the right people, get out of their way to run their business and make sure successors are identified
- **Lesson #2** - Back yourself, even when your ideas and beliefs are controversial or counter-intuitive
- **Lesson #3** - As a leader you set the culture for the business and the right culture is a valuable and hard-to-replicate source of advantage.
- **Lesson #4** - Having a passion, purpose and long-term perspective helps avoid taking risks for short-term gain
- **Lesson #5** - He communicates in a way that we can all understand

5. **Starbucks** – The Corporate Mission Statement from the Starbucks website follows:

Our Starbucks Mission Statement

Our mission: to inspire and nurture the human spirit – one person, one cup and one neighborhood at a time.

Here are the principles of how we live that every day:

Our Coffee

It has always been, and will always be, about quality. We're passionate about ethically sourcing the finest coffee beans, roasting them with great care, and improving the lives of people who grow them. We care deeply about all of this; our work is never done.

Our Partners

We're called partners, because it's not just a job, it's our passion. Together, we embrace diversity to create a place where each of us can be ourselves. We always treat each other with respect and dignity. And we hold each other to that standard.

Our Customers

When we are fully engaged, we connect with, laugh with, and uplift the lives of our customers – even if just for a few moments. Sure, it starts with the promise of a perfectly made beverage, but our work goes far beyond that. It's really about human connection.

Our Stores

When our customers feel this sense of belonging, our stores become a haven, a break from the worries outside, a place where you can meet with friends. It's about enjoyment at the speed of life – sometimes slow and savored, sometimes faster. Always full of humanity.

Our Neighborhood

Every store is part of a community, and we take our responsibility to be good neighbors seriously. We want to be invited in wherever we do business. We can be a force for positive action – bringing together our partners, customers, and the community to contribute every day. Now we see that our responsibility – and our potential for good – is even larger. The world is looking to Starbucks to set the new standard, yet again. We will lead.

Our Shareholders

*We know that as we deliver in each of these areas, we enjoy the kind of success that rewards our shareholders. We are fully accountable to get each of these elements right so that Starbucks – **and everyone it touches** – **can endure and thrive.***

Thankfully, respect and admiration also mean higher profits as indicated by the information in the table below. Over the past 10 years the stock price of the top 50 companies on the World's Most Admired Companies (WMAC) list have outperformed the S&P 500 by over five times:

Total Shareholder Returns		
	WMAC	**S&P 500**
One Year	22.6%	15.1%
Three Years	4.3%	-2.8%
Five Years	8.3%	2.3%
Ten Years	7.8%	1.4%

Hopefully, you were able to recognize a lot of the attributes from The Pyramid of Business Success in the corporate mission statements and management philosophies of the most admired companies in the world. Believe me, if these organizations can abide and thrive by these principles then every other business owner/manager can as well. It simply takes a desire and passion to make it happen.

The elements in The Pyramid of Business Success can be used as part of an introductory meeting with potential clients to introduce the values important to you and your business. Hopefully, your message will also resonate with your potential customers and it could be a deciding factor in their purchasing decision, ESPECIALLY if they see that you truly operate your business by these principles.

It is up to you as a business owner/manager to determine what type of company you want to build. If you are interested in creating a business that is profitable, that cares about your people and that is focused on long term success then this book will help.

I wish you all the best of luck!!

"Knowledge without application is like a book that is never read"
– Christopher Crawford

"...to learn and not to do is really not to learn. To know and not to do is really not to know." - **Stephen R. Covey**

287

"Man's greatness consists in his ability to "do", and the proper application of his powers to things needed to be done." - **Frederick Douglass**

My deepest thanks and gratitude go to my beautiful and creative wife Anne Marie. Without your support and help, this book would never have been possible.

A special thank you is also owed to my friends and family that took the time to offer me their thoughts and guidance. Your feedback was extremely valuable and it helped to make this book much better than I would have been able to do simply by my own efforts.

I am truly lucky!